Grasmere Edition

THE COMPLETE POETICAL WORKS

OF

WILLIAM WORDSWORTH

IN TEN VOLUMES

VOLUME X

Ætat 77

THE COMPLETE POETICAL

WORKS OF

WILLIAM WORDSWORTH 1770-1850

X

PREFATORY ESSAYS
AND NOTES

BOSTON AND NEW YORK

HOUGHTON MIFFLIN COMPANY

1911

CONTENTS

NOTES ON THE ILLUSTRATIONS

[vii]

NOTES ON THE ILLUSTRATIONS

"One of thy lowly dwellings is my home."

Wordsworth's home at Grasmere from 1799 to 1808, where most of his best work was done.

PREFACES, POSTSCRIPTS, NOTES, INDEXES, ETC.

PREFACES, POSTSCRIPTS, NOTES, INDEXES, ETC.

PREFACE [1]

1800

MUCH the greatest part of the foregoing Poems has been so long before the Public that no prefatory matter, explanatory of any portion of them or of the arrangement which has been adopted, appears to be required; and had it not been for the observations contained in those Prefaces upon the principle of Poetry in general, they would not have been reprinted even as an Appendix in this Edition.

PREFACE

TO THE SECOND EDITION OF SEVERAL OF THE FOREGOING POEMS, PUBLISHED, WITH AN ADDITIONAL VOLUME, UNDER THE TITLE OF "LYRICAL BALLADS"

Note. — In succeeding Editions, when the Collection was much enlarged and diversified, this Preface was transferred to the end of the Volumes as having little of a special application to their contents.

The first volume of these Poems has already been submitted to general perusal. It was published as an experiment, which, I hoped, might be of some use to

---

[1] The ideas which were expanded into the following Prefaces and

ascertain how far, by fitting to metrical arrangement
a selection of the real language of men in a state of vivid
sensation, that sort of pleasure and that quantity of
pleasure, may be imparted, which a Poet may ration-
ally endeavour to impart.

I had formed no very inaccurate estimate of the probable effect of those Poems: I flattered myself that they
who should be pleased with them would read them
with more than common pleasure: and, on the other
hand, I was well aware, that by those who should dislike them they would be read with more than common
dislike. The result has differed from my expectation
in this only, that a greater number have been pleased
than I ventured to hope I should please.

. . . .

Several of my Friends are anxious for the success
of these Poems, from a belief that, if the views with
which they were composed were indeed realised, a class
of Poetry would be produced, well adapted to interest
mankind permanently, and not unimportant in the
quality and in the multiplicity of its moral relations:
and on this account they have advised me to prefix
a systematic defence of the theory upon which the
Poems were written. But I was unwilling to under-

Essays first appeared as a Preface to the second edition of the *Lyrical Ballads,* 1800. In the edition of 1802 the Preface to that of 1800
was enlarged, and there was added an Appendix on "Poetic Diction."
These were repeated in successive editions of the poet's works —
with alterations, insertions, and omissions — until they received
their last revision in the Edition of 1845. — ED.

take the task, knowing that on this occasion the Reader would look coldly upon my arguments, since I might be suspected of having been principally influenced by the selfish and foolish hope of *reasoning* him into an approbation of these particular Poems: and I was still more unwilling to undertake the task, because adequately to display the opinions, and fully to enforce the arguments, would require a space wholly disproportionate to a preface. For, to treat the subject with the clearness and coherence of which it is susceptible, it would be necessary to give a full account of the present state of the public taste in this country, and to determine how far this taste is healthy or depraved; which, again, could not be determined without pointing out in what manner language and the human mind act and re-act on each other, and without retracing the revolutions, not of literature alone, but likewise of society itself. I have therefore altogether declined to enter regularly upon this defence; yet I am sensible that there would be something like impropriety in abruptly obtruding upon the Public, without a few words of introduction, Poems so materially different from those upon which general approbation is at present bestowed.

It is supposed that by the act of writing in verse an Author makes a formal engagement that he will gratify certain known habits of association; that he not only thus apprises the Reader that certain classes of ideas and expressions will be found in his book, but that others will be carefully excluded. This exponent or symbol held forth by metrical language must in different eras of literature have excited very different expectations: for example, in the age of Catullus, Terence, and Lucretius, and that of Statius or Claudian; and in our own country, in the age of Shakespeare and Beaumont and Fletcher, and that of Donne and Cowley, or Dryden, or Pope. I will not take upon me to determine the exact import of the promise which, by the act of writing in verse, an Author in the present day makes to his reader; but it will undoubtedly appear to many persons that I have not fulfilled the terms of an engagement thus voluntarily contracted. They who have been accustomed to the gaudiness and inane phraseology of many modern writers, if they persist in reading this book to its conclusion, will, no doubt, frequently have to struggle with feelings of strangeness and awkwardness: they will look round for poetry, and will be induced to inquire by what species of courtesy these attempts can be permitted to assume that title. I hope, therefore, the reader will not censure me for attempting to state what I have proposed to myself to perform; and also (as far as the limits of a preface will permit) to explain some of the chief reasons which have determined me in the choice of my purpose: that at least he may be spared any unpleasant feeling of disappointment, and that I myself may be protected from one of the most dishonourable accusations which can be brought against an Author; namely, that of an indolence which prevents him from endeavouring to ascertain what is his duty, or, when his duty is ascertained, prevents him from performing it.

The principal object, then, proposed in these Poems, was to choose incidents and situations from common life, and to relate or describe them throughout, as far as was possible, in a selection of language really used by men, and, at the same time, to throw over them a certain colouring of imagination, whereby ordinary things should be presented to the mind in an unusual aspect; and further, and above all, to make these incidents and situations interesting by tracing in them, truly though not ostentatiously, the primary laws of our nature: chiefly, as far as regards the manner in which we associate ideas in a state of excitement. Humble and rustic life was generally chosen, because in that condition the essential passions of the heart find a better soil in which they can attain their maturity, are less under restraint, and speak a plainer and more emphatic language; because in that condition of life our elementary feelings co-exist in a state of greater simplicity, and, consequently, may be more accurately contemplated, and more forcibly communicated; because the manners of rural life germinate from those elementary feelings, and, from the necessary character of rural occupations, are more easily comprehended, and are more durable; and, lastly, because in that condition the passions of men are incorporated with the beautiful and permanent forms of nature. The language, too, of these men has been adopted (purified indeed from what appear to be its real defects, from all lasting and rational causes of dislike or disgust), because such men hourly communicate with the best objects from which the best part of language is originally derived; and because, from their rank in society and the sameness and narrow circle of their intercourse, being less under the influence of social vanity, they convey their feelings and notions in simple and unelaborated expressions. Accordingly, such a language, arising out of repeated experience and regular feelings, is a more permanent, and a far more philosophical language, than that which is frequently substituted for it by Poets, who think that they are conferring honour upon themselves and their art in proportion as they separate themselves from the sympathies of men, and indulge in arbitrary and capricious habits of expression, in order to furnish food for fickle tastes and fickle appetites of their own creation.[1]

I cannot, however, be insensible to the present outcry against the triviality and meanness, both of thought and language, which some of my contemporaries have occasionally introduced into their metrical compositions; and I acknowledge that this defect, where it exists, is more dishonourable to the Writer's own character than false refinement or arbitrary innovation,

[1] It is worth while here to observe that the affecting parts of Chaucer are almost always expressed in language pure and universally intelligible even to this day.

though I should contend at the same time that it is far less pernicious in the sum of its consequences. From such verses the Poems in these volumes will be found distinguished at least by one mark of difference, that each of them has a worthy *purpose*. Not that I always began to write with a distinct purpose formally conceived, but habits of meditation have, I trust, so prompted and regulated my feelings, that my descriptions of such objects as strongly excite those feelings will be found to carry along with them a *purpose*. If this opinion be erroneous, I can have little right to the name of a Poet. For all good poetry is the spontaneous overflow of powerful feelings: and though this be true, Poems to which any value can be attached were never produced on any variety of subjects but by a man who, being possessed of more than usual organic sensibility, had also thought long and deeply. For our continued influxes of feeling are modified and directed by our thoughts, which are indeed the representatives of all our past feelings; and as, by contemplating the relation of these general representatives to each other, we discover what is really important to men, so, by the repetition and continuance of this act, our feelings will be connected with important subjects, till at length, if we be originally possessed of much sensibility, such habits of mind will be produced that, by obeying blindly and mechanically the impulses of those habits, we shall describe objects, and utter sentiments, of such a nature, and in such connection with each other, that the understanding of the Reader must necessarily be in some degree enlightened, and his affection strengthened and purified.

It has been said that each of these Poems has a purpose. Another circumstance must be mentioned which distinguishes these Poems from the popular Poetry of the day; it is this, that the feeling therein developed gives importance to the action and situation, and not the action and situation to the feeling.

A sense of false modesty shall not prevent me from asserting that the Reader's attention is pointed to this mark of distinction, far less for the sake of these particular Poems than from the general importance of the subject. The subject is indeed important! For the human mind is capable of being excited without the application of gross and violent stimulants; and he must have a very faint perception of its beauty and dignity who does not know this, and who does not further know, that one being is elevated above another in proportion as he possesses this capability. It has therefore appeared to me, that to endeavour to produce or enlarge this capability is one of the best services in which, at any period, a Writer can be engaged; but this service, excellent at all times, is especially so at the present day. For a multitude of causes, unknown to former times, are now acting with a combined force to blunt the discriminating powers of the mind, and, unfitting it for all voluntary exertion, to reduce it to a state of almost savage torpor. The most effective of these causes are the great national events which are daily taking place, and the increasing accumulation of men in cities, where the uniformity of their occupations produces a craving for extraordinary incident which the rapid communication of intelligence hourly gratifies. To this tendency of life and manners the literature and theatrical exhibitions of the country have conformed themselves. The invaluable works of our elder writers, I had almost said the works of Shakespeare and Milton, are driven into neglect by frantic novels, sickly and stupid German Tragedies, and deluges of idle and extravagant stories in verse. — When I think upon this degrading thirst after outrageous stimulation, I am almost ashamed to have spoken of the feeble endeavour made in these volumes to counteract it; and, reflecting upon the magnitude of the general evil, I should be oppressed with no dishonourable melancholy, had I not a deep impression of certain inherent and indestructible qualities of the human mind, and likewise of certain powers in the great and permanent objects that act upon it, which are equally inherent and indestructible; and were there not added to this impression a belief that the time is approaching when the evil will be systematically opposed by men of greater powers, and with far more distinguished success.

Having dwelt thus long on the subjects and aim of these Poems, I shall request the Reader's permission to apprise him of a few circumstances relating to their *style*, in order, among other reasons, that he may not censure me for not having performed what I never attempted. The Reader will find that personifications of abstract ideas rarely occur in these volumes, and are utterly rejected as an ordinary device to elevate the style and raise it above prose. My purpose was to imitate, and, as far as is possible, to adopt the very language of men; and assuredly such personifications do not make any natural or regular part of that language. They are, indeed, a figure of speech occasionally prompted by passion, and I have made use of them as such; but have endeavoured utterly to reject them as a mechanical devise of style, or as a family language which Writers in metre seem to lay claim to by prescription. I have wished to keep the Reader in the company of flesh and blood, persuaded that by so doing I shall interest him. Others who pursue a different track will interest him likewise; I do not interfere with their claim, but wish to prefer a claim of my own. There will also be found in these volumes little of what is usually called poetic diction; as much pains has been taken to avoid it as is ordinarily taken to produce it; this has been done for the reason already alleged, to bring my language near to the language of men; and further, because the pleasure which I have proposed to myself to impart is of a kind very different from that which is supposed by many persons to be the proper object of poetry. Without being culpably particular, I do not know how to give my Reader a more exact notion of the style in which it was my wish and intention to write, than by informing him that I have at all times endeavoured to look steadily at my subject; consequently there is, I hope, in these Poems little falsehood of description, and my ideas are expressed in language fitted to their respective importance. Something must have been gained by this practice, as it is friendly to one property of all good poetry, namely, good sense: but it has necessarily cut me off from a large portion of phrases and figures of speech which from father to son have long been regarded as the common inheritance of Poets. I have also thought it expedient to restrict myself still further, having abstained from the use of many expressions, in themselves proper and beautiful, but which have been foolishly repeated by bad Poets, till such feelings of disgust are connected with them as it is scarcely possible by any art of association to overpower.

If in a poem there should be found a series of lines, or even a single line, in which the language, though naturally arranged, and according to the strict laws of metre, does not differ from that of prose, there is a numerous class of critics, who, when they stumble upon these prosaisms, as they call them, imagine that they have made a notable discovery, and exult over the Poet as over a man ignorant of his own profession. Now these men would establish a canon of criticism which the Reader will conclude he must utterly reject, if he wishes to be pleased with these volumes. And it would be a most easy task to prove to him that not only the language of a large portion of every good

poem, even of the most elevated character, must necessarily, except with reference to the metre, in no respect
differ from that of good prose, but likewise that some
of the most interesting parts of the best poems will be
found to be strictly the language of prose when prose
is well written. The truth of this assertion might be
demonstrated by innumerable passages from almost
all the poetical writings, even of Milton himself. To
illustrate the subject in a general manner, I will here
adduce a short composition of Gray, who was at the
head of those who, by their reasonings, have attempted
to widen the space of separation betwixt Prose and
Metrical composition, and was more than any other
man curiously elaborate in the structure of his own
poetic diction.

> "In vain to me the smiling mornings shine,
> And reddening Phœbus lifts his golden fire;
> The birds in vain their amorous descant join,
> Or cheerful fields resume their green attire.
> These ears, alas! for other notes repine;
> *A different object do these eyes require ;*
> *My lonely anguish melts no heart but mine ;*
> *And in my breast the imperfect joys expire ;*
> Yet morning smiles the busy race to cheer,
> And new-born pleasure brings to happier men;
> The fields to all their wonted tribute bear;
> To warm their little loves the birds complain.
> *I fruitless mourn to him that cannot hear,*
> *And weep the more because I weep in vain."*

It will easily be perceived, that the only part of this
Sonnet which is of any value is the lines printed in

Italics; it is equally obvious that, except in the rhyme
and in the use of the single word "fruitless" for fruit-
lessly, which is so far a defect, the language of these
lines does in no respect differ from that of prose.

By the foregoing quotation it has been shown that the
language of Prose may yet be well adapted to Poetry;
and it was previously asserted that a large portion of
the language of every good poem can in no respect differ
from that of good Prose. We will go further. It may be
safely affirmed that there neither is, nor can be, any
essential difference between the language of prose and
metrical composition. We are fond of tracing the resemblance between Poetry and Painting, and, accordingly, we call them Sisters: but where shall we find bonds
of connection sufficiently strict to typify the affinity
betwixt metrical and prose composition? They both
speak by and to the same organs; the bodies in which
both of them are clothed may be said to be of the same
substance, their affections are kindred, and almost
identical, not necessarily differing even in degree;
Poetry [1] sheds no tears "such as Angels weep," but

---

[1] I here use the word "Poetry" (though against my own judgment)
as opposed to the word Prose, and synonymous with metrical
composition. But much confusion has been introduced into criticism
by this contradistinction of Poetry and Prose, instead of the more
philosophical one of Poetry and Matter of Fact, or Science. The only
strict antithesis to Prose is Metre; nor is this, in truth, a *strict* antithesis, because lines and passages of metre so naturally occur in
writing prose, that it would be scarcely possible to avoid them, even
were it desirable.

natural and human tears; she can boast of no celestial
ichor that distinguishes her vital juices from those of
Prose; the same human blood circulates through the
veins of them both.

If it be affirmed that rhyme and metrical arrangement of themselves constitute a distinction which over-
turns what has just been said on the strict affinity of
metrical language with that of Prose, and paves the
way for other artificial distinctions which the mind
voluntarily admits, I answer that the language of such
Poetry as is here recommended is, as far as is possible,
a selection of the language really spoken by men; that
this selection, wherever it is made with true taste and
feeling, will of itself form a distinction far greater than
would at first be imagined, and will entirely separate
the composition from the vulgarity and meanness of
ordinary life; and, if metre be superadded thereto, I believe that a dissimilitude will be produced altogether
sufficient for the gratification of a rational mind. What
other distinction would we have? Whence is it to come?
And where is it to exist? Not, surely, where the Poet
speaks through the mouths of his characters: it cannot
be necessary here, either for elevation of style, or any of
its supposed ornaments; for, if the Poet's subject be
judiciously chosen, it will naturally, and upon fit occasion, lead him to passions, the language of which, if selected truly and judiciously, must necessarily be dignified and variegated, and alive with metaphors and
figures. I forbear to speak of an incongruity which would

shock the intelligent Reader, should the Poet inter-
weave any foreign splendour of his own with that which
the passion naturally suggests: it is sufficient to say
that such addition is unnecessary. And, surely, it is
more probable that those passages, which with propriety
abound with metaphors and figures, will have their due
effect if, upon other occasions where the passions are of a
milder character, the style also be subdued and temperate.

But, as the pleasure which I hope to give by the
Poems now presented to the Reader must depend entirely on just notions upon this subject, and as it is in
itself of high importance to our taste and moral feelings,
I cannot content myself with these detached remarks.
And if, in what I am about to say, it shall appear to
some that my labour is unnecessary, and that I am like
a man fighting a battle without enemies, such persons
may be reminded that, whatever be the language outwardly holden by men, a practical faith in the opinions
which I am wishing to establish is almost unknown. If
my conclusions are admitted, and carried as far as they
must be carried if admitted at all, our judgments concerning the works of the greatest Poets, both ancient
and modern, will be far different from what they are
at present, both when we praise and when we censure:
and our moral feelings influencing and influenced by
these judgments will, I believe, be corrected and purified.

Taking up the subject, then, upon general grounds,

[17]

let me ask, what is meant by the word Poet? What is a Poet? To whom does he address himself? And what language is to be expected from him? — He is a man speaking to men: a man, it is true, endowed with more lively sensibility, more enthusiasm and tenderness, who has a greater knowledge of human nature, and a more comprehensive soul, than are supposed to be common among mankind; a man pleased with his own passions, and volitions, and who rejoices more than other men in the spirit of life that is in him; delighting to contemplate similar volitions and passions as manifested in the goings-on of the Universe, and habitually impelled to create them where he does not find them. To these qualities he has added a disposition to be affected more than any other men by absent things as if they were present; an ability of cojnuring up in himself passions, which are indeed far from being the same as those produced by real events, yet (especially in those parts of the general sympathy which are pleasing and delightful) do more nearly resemble the passions produced by real events than anything which, from the motions of their own minds merely, other men are accustomed to feel in themselves: — whence, and from practice, he has acquired a greater readiness and power in expressing what he thinks and feels, and especially those thoughts and feelings which, by his own choice, or from the structure of his own mind, arise in him without the immediate external excitement.

But whatever portion of this faculty we may suppose

even the greatest Poet to possess, there cannot be a doubt that the language which it will suggest to him must often, in liveliness and truth, fall short of that which is uttered by men in real life under the actual pressure of those passions, certain shadows of which the Poet thus produces, or feels to be produced, in himself.

However exalted a notion we would wish to cherish of the character of a Poet, it is obvious that, while he describes and imitates passions, his employment is in some degree mechanical compared with the freedom and power of real and substantial action and suffering. So that it will be the wish of the Poet to bring his feelings near to those of the persons whose feelings he describes, nay, for short spaces of time, perhaps, to let himself slip into an entire delusion, and even confound and identify his own feelings with theirs; modifying only the language which is thus suggested to him by a consideration that he describes for a particular purpose, that of giving pleasure. Here, then, he will apply the principle of selection which has been already insisted upon. He will depend upon this for removing what would otherwise be painful or disgusting in the passion; he will feel that there is no necessity to trick out or to elevate nature: and the more industriously he applies this principle the deeper will be his faith that no words, which *his* fancy or imagination can suggest, will be to be compared with those which are the emanations of reality and truth.

But it may be said by those who do not object to
the general spirit of these remarks, that, as it is impossible for the Poet to produce upon all occasions language as exquisitely fitted for the passion as that
which the real passion itself suggests, it is proper that
he should consider himself as in the situation of a translator, who does not scruple to substitute excellences of
another kind for those which are unattainable by him;
and endeavours occasionally to surpass his original, in
order to make some amends for the general inferiority
to which he feels he must submit. But this would be
to encourage idleness and unmanly despair. Further,
it is the language of men who speak of what they do not
understand; who talk of Poetry, as of a matter of amusement and idle pleasure; who will converse with us as
gravely about a *taste* for Poetry, as they express it, as
if it were a thing as indifferent as a taste for rope-danc-
ing, or Frontiniac or Sherry. Aristotle, I have been
told, has said, that Poetry is the most philosophic of
all writing: it is so: its object is truth, not individual
and local, but general and operative; not standing upon
external testimony, but carried alive into the heart by
passion; truth which is its own testimony, which gives
competence and confidence to the tribunal to which
it appeals, and receives them from the same tribunal.
Poetry is the image of man and nature. The obstacles
which stand in the way of the fidelity of the Biographer
and Historian, and of their consequent utility, are in-
calculably greater than those which are to be encoun-

tered by the Poet who comprehends the dignity of his art. The Poet writes under one restriction only, namely, the necessity of giving immediate pleasure to a human Being possessed of that information which may be expected from him, not as a lawyer, a physician, a mariner, an astronomer, or a natural philosopher, but as a Man. Except this one restriction, there is no object standing between the Poet and the image of things; between this, and the Biographer and Historian, there are a thousand.

Nor let this necessity of producing immediate pleasure be considered as a degradation of the Poet's art. It is far otherwise. It is an acknowledgment of the beauty of the universe, an acknowledgment the more sincere because not formal, but indirect; it is a task light and easy to him who looks at the world in the spirit of love: further, it is a homage paid to the native and naked dignity of man, to the grand elementary principle of pleasure, by which he knows, and feels, and lives, and moves. We have no sympathy but what is propagated by pleasure: I would not be misunderstood; but wherever we sympathise with pain, it will be found that the sympathy is produced and carried on by subtle combinations with pleasure. We have no knowledge, that is, no general principles drawn from the contemplation of particular facts, but what has been built up by pleasure, and exists in us by pleasure alone. The Man of science, the Chemist and Mathematician, whatever difficulties and disgusts they may have had to struggle with, know and feel this. However painful may be the objects with which the Anatomist's knowledge is connected, he feels that his knowledge is pleasure; and where he has no pleasure he has no knowledge. What then does the Poet? He considers man and the objects that surround him as acting and re-acting upon each other, so as to produce an infinite complexity of pain and pleasure; he considers man in his own nature and in his ordinary life as contemplating this with a certain quantity of immediate knowledge, with certain convictions, intuitions, and deductions, which from habit acquire the quality of intuitions; he considers him as looking upon this complex scene of ideas and sensations, and finding everywhere objects that immediately excite in him sympathies, which from the necessities of his nature, are accompanied by an overbalance of enjoyment.

To this knowledge which all men carry about with them, and to these sympathies in which, without any other discipline than that of our daily life, we are fitted to take delight, the Poet principally directs his attention. He considers man and nature as essentially adapted to each other, and the mind of man as naturally the mirror of the fairest amd most interesting properties of nature. And thus the Poet, prompted by this feeling of pleasure, which accompanies him through the whole course of his studies, converses with general nature, with affections akin to those which, through labour and length of time, the Man of science has raised up in himself, by conversing with those particular parts of na-

ture which are the objects of his studies. The knowledge
both of the Poet and the Man of science is pleasure;
but the knowledge of the one cleaves to us as a necessary part of our existence, our natural and unalienable
inheritance; the other is a personal and individual ac-
quisition, slow to come to us, and by no habitual and
direct sympathy connecting us with our fellow-beings.
The Man of science seeks truth as a remote and unknown benefactor; he cherishes and loves it in his solitude: the Poet, singing a song in which all human beings
join with him, rejoices in the presence of truth as our
visible friend and hourly companion. Poetry is the
breath and finer spirit of all knowledge; it is the impassioned expression which is in the countenance of all
Science. Emphatically may it be said of the Poet, as
Shakespeare hath said of man, "that he looks before and
after." He is the rock of defence for human nature; an
upholder and preserver, carrying everywhere with
him relationship and love. In spite of difference of soil
and climate, of language and manners, of laws and customs: in spite of things silently gone out of mind, and
things violently destroyed; the Poet binds together by
passion and knowledge the vast empire of human society, as it is spread over the whole earth and over all
time. The objects of the Poet's thoughts are everywhere;
though the eyes and senses of man are, it is true, his
favourite guides, yet he will follow wheresoever he can
find an atmosphere of sensation in which to move his
wings. Poetry is the first and last of all knowledge —

it is as immortal as the heart of man. If the labours of Men of science should ever create any material revolution, direct or indirect, in our condition, and in the impressions which we habitually receive, the Poet will sleep then no more than at present; he will be ready to follow the steps of the Man of science, not only in those general indirect effects, but he will be at his side, carrying sensation into the midst of the objects of the science itself. The remotest discoveries of the Chemist, the Botanist, or Mineralogist, will be as proper objects of the Poet's art as any upon which it can be employed, if the time should ever come when these things shall be familiar to us, and the relations under which they are contemplated by the followers of these respective sciences shall be manifestly and palpably material to us as enjoying and suffering beings. If the time should ever come when what is now called science, thus familiarised to men, shall be ready to put on, as it were, a form of flesh and blood, the Poet will lend his divine spirit to aid the transfiguration, and will welcome the Being thus produced as a dear and genuine inmate of the household of man. — It is not, then, to be supposed that any one, who holds that sublime notion of Poetry which I have attempted to convey, will break in upon the sanctity and truth of his pictures by transitory and accidental ornaments, and endeavour to excite admiration of himself by arts, the necessity of which must manifestly depend upon the assumed meanness of his subject.

PREFACE

What has been thus far said applies to Poetry in general, but especially to those parts of compositions where the Poet speaks through the mouths of his characters; and upon this point it appears to authorise the conclusion that there are few persons of good sense who would not allow that the dramatic parts of composition are defective in proportion as they deviate from the real language of nature, and are coloured by a diction of the Poet's own, either peculiar to him as an individual Poet or belonging simply to Poets in general; to a body of men who, from the circumstance of their compositions being in metre, it is expected will employ a particular language.

It is not, then, in the dramatic parts of composition that we look for this distinction of language; but still it may be proper and necessary where the Poet speaks to us in his own person and character. To this I answer by referring the Reader to the description before given of a Poet. Among the qualities there enumerated as principally conducing to form a Poet, is implied nothing differing in kind from other men, but only in degree. The sum of what was said is, that the Poet is chiefly distinguished from other men by a greater promptness to think and feel without immediate external excitement, and a greater power in expressing such thoughts and feelings as are produced in him in that manner. But these passions and thoughts and feelings are the general passions and thoughts and feelings of men. And with what are they connected? Undoubtedly with our moral

sentiments and animal sensations, and with the causes
which excite these; with the operations of the elements,
and the appearances of the visible universe; with storm
and sunshine, with the revolutions of the seasons, with
cold and heat, with loss of friends and kindred, with
injuries and resentments, gratitude and hope, with fear
and sorrow. These, and the like, are the sensations and
objects which the Poet describes, as they are the sensations of other men and the objects which interest
them. The Poet thinks and feels in the spirit of human
passions. How, then, can his language differ in any material degree from that of all other men who feel vividly
and see clearly? It might be *proved* that it is impossible. But supposing that this were not the case, the
Poet might then be allowed to use a peculiar language
when expressing his feelings for his own gratification,
or that of men like himself. But Poets do not write for
Poets alone, but for men. Unless, therefore, we are
advocates for that admiration which subsists upon
ignorance, and that pleasure which arises from hearing
what we do not understand, the Poet must descend
from this supposed height; and, in order to excite rational sympathy, he must express himself as other men
express themselves. To this it may be added, that
while he is only selecting from the real language of men,
or, which amounts to the same thing, composing accurately in the spirit of such selection, he is treading upon
safe ground, and we know what we are to expect from
him. Our feelings are the same with respect to metre;

for, as it may be proper to remind the Reader, the distinction of metre is regular and uniform, and not, like that which is produced by what is usually called POETIC DICTION, arbitrary, and subject to infinite caprices, upon which no calculation whatever can be made. In the one case, the Reader is utterly at the mercy of the Poet, respecting what imagery or diction he may choose to connect with the passion; whereas, in the other, the metre obeys certain laws, to which the Poet and Reader both willingly submit because they are certain, and because no interference is made by them with the passion but such as the concurring testimony of ages has shown to heighten and improve the pleasure which co-exists with it.

It will now be proper to answer an obvious question, namely, Why, professing these opinions, have I written in verse? To this, in addition to such answer as is included in what has been already said, I reply, in the first place, Because, however I may have restricted myself, there is still left open to me what confessedly constitutes the most valuable object of all writing, whether in prose or verse; the great and universal passions of men, the most general and interesting of their occupations, and the entire world of nature before me — to supply endless combinations of forms and imagery. Now, supposing for a moment that whatever is interesting in these objects may be as vividly described in prose, why should I be condemned for attempting to superadd to such description the charm which, by the

consent of all nations, is acknowledged to exist in metrical language? To this, by such as are yet unconvinced,
it may be answered that a very small part of the pleasure given by Poetry depends upon the metre, and that
it is injudicious to write in metre, unless it be accompanied with the other artificial distinctions of style
with which metre is usually accompanied, and that,
by such deviation, more will be lost from the shock
which will thereby be given to the Reader's associations
than will be counterbalanced by any pleasure which he
can derive from the general power of numbers. In answer
to those who still contend for the necessity of accompanying metre with certain appropriate colours of
style in order to the accomplishment of its appropriate
end, and who also, in my opinion, greatly under-rate
the power of metre in itself, it might, perhaps, as far as
relates to these Volumes, have been almost sufficient
to observe, that poems are extant, written upon more
humble subjects, and in a still more naked and simple
style, which have continued to give pleasure from generation to generation. Now, if nakedness and simplicity
be a defect, the fact here mentioned affords a strong
presumption that poems somewhat less naked and simple
are capable of affording pleasure at the present day; and,
what I wished *chiefly* to attempt, at present, was to justify myself for having written under the impression
of this belief.

But various causes might be pointed out why, when
the style is manly, and the subject of some importance,

words metrically arranged will long continue to impart
such a pleasure to mankind as he who proves the extent
of that pleasure will be desirous to impart. The end
of poetry is to produce excitement in co-existence with
an overbalance of pleasure; but, by the supposition,
excitement is an unusual and irregular state of the mind;
ideas and feelings do not, in that state, succeed each
other in accustomed order. If the words, however, by
which this excitement is produced be in themselves
powerful, or the images and feelings have an undue
proportion of pain connected with them, there is some
danger that the excitement may be carried beyond its
proper bounds. Now the co-presence of something
regular, something to which the mind has been accustomed in various moods and in a less excited state, cannot but have great efficacy in tempering and restrain-
ing the passion by an intertexture of ordinary feeling,
and of feeling not strictly and necessarily connected
with the passion. This is unquestionably true; and hence,
though the opinion will at first appear paradoxical,
from the tendency of metre to divest language, in a
certain degree, of its reality, and thus to throw a sort
of half-consciousness of unsubstantial existence over
the whole composition, there can be little doubt but that
more pathetic situations and sentiments, that is, those
which have a greater proportion of pain connected
with them, may be endured in metrical composition,
especially in rhyme, than in prose. The metre of the
old ballads is very artless, yet they contain many pas-

sages which would illustrate this opinion; and, I hope, if the following poems be attentively perused, similar instances will be found in them. This opinion may be further illustrated by appealing to the Reader's own experience of the reluctance with which he comes to the reperusal of the distressful parts of "Clarissa Harlowe," or the "Gamester"; while Shakspeare's writings, in the most pathetic scenes, never act upon us as pathetic, beyond the bounds of pleasure — an effect which, in a much greater degree than might at first be imagined, is to be ascribed to small, but continual and regular impulses of pleasurable surprise from the metrical arrangement. — On the other hand (what it must be allowed will much more frequently happen), if the Poet's words should be incommensurate with the passion, and inadequate to raise the Reader to a height of desirable excitement, then (unless the Poet's choice of his metre has been grossly injudicious), in the feelings of pleasure which the Reader has been accustomed to connect with metre in general, and in the feeling, whether cheerful or melancholy, which he has been accustomed to connect with that particular movement of metre, there will be found something which will greatly contribute to impart passion to the words, and to effect the complex end which the Poet proposes to himself.

If I had undertaken a SYSTEMATIC defence of the theory here maintained, it would have been my duty to develop the various causes upon which the pleasure received from metrical language depends. Among the chief of these causes is to be reckoned a principle which must be well known to those who have made any of the Arts the object of accurate reflection; namely, the pleasure which the mind derives from the perception of similitude in dissimilitude. This principle is the great spring of the activity of our minds, and their chief feeder. From this principle the direction of the sexual appetite, and all the passions connected with it, take their origin: it is the life of our ordinary conversation; and upon the accuracy with which similitude in dissimilitude, and dissimilitude in similitude, are perceived, depend our taste and our moral feelings. It would not be a useless employment to apply this principle to the consideration of metre, and to show that metre is hence enabled to afford much pleasure, and to point out in what manner that pleasure is produced. But my limits will not permit me to enter upon this subject, and I must content myself with a general summary.

I have said that poetry is the spontaneous overflow of powerful feelings: it takes its origin from emotion recollected in tranquillity; the emotion is contemplated till, by a species of re-action, the tranquillity gradually disappears, and an emotion, kindred to that which was before the subject of contemplation, is gradually produced, and does itself actually exist in the mind. In this mood successful composition generally begins, and in a mood similar to this it is carried on; but the emotion, of whatever kind, and in whatever degree, from various causes, is qualified by various pleasures, so that in describing any passions whatsoever, which are voluntarily described, the mind will, upon the whole, be in a state of enjoyment. If Nature be thus cautious to preserve in a state of enjoyment a being so employed, the Poet ought to profit by the lesson held forth to him, and ought especially to take care that, whatever passions he communicates to his Reader, those passions, if his Reader's mind be sound and vigorous, should always be accompanied with an over-balance of pleasure. Now the music of harmonious metrical language, the sense of difficulty overcome, and the blind association of pleasure which has been previously received from works of rhyme or metre of the same or similar construction, an indistinct perception perpetually renewed of language closely resembling that of real life, and yet, in the circumstance of metre, differing from it so widely — all these imperceptibly make up a complex feeling of delight, which is of the most important use in tempering the painful feeling always found intermingled with powerful descriptions of the deeper passions. This effect is always produced in pathetic and impassioned poetry; while, in lighter compositions, the ease and gracefulness with which the Poet manages his numbers are themselves confessedly a principal source of the gratification of the Reader. All that it is *necessary* to say, however, upon this subject, may be effected by affirming, what few persons will deny, that of two descriptions, either of passions, manners, or characters, each of them equally well executed, the one in prose and the other in verse, the verse will be read a hundred times where the prose is read once.

Having thus explained a few of my reasons for writing in verse, and why I have chosen subjects from common life, and endeavoured to bring my language near to the real language of men, if I have been too minute in pleading my own cause, I have at the same time been treating a subject of general interest; and for this reason a few words shall be added with reference solely to these particular poems, and to some defects which will probably be found in them. I am sensible that my associations must have sometimes been particular instead of general, and that, consequently, giving to things a false importance, I may have sometimes written upon unworthy subjects; but I am less apprehensive on this account, than that my language may frequently have suffered from those arbitrary connections of feelings and ideas with particular words and phrases from which no man can altogether protect himself. Hence I have no doubt that, in some instances, feelings, even of the ludicrous, may be given to my Readers by expressions which appeared to me tender and pathetic. Such faulty expressions, were I convinced they were faulty at present, and that they must necessarily continue to be so, I would willingly take all reasonable pains to correct. But it is dangerous to make these alterations on the simple authority of a few individuals, or even of certain classes of men; for where the understanding of an author is not convinced, or his feelings altered, this cannot be done without great injury to himself: for his own feelings are his stay and support; and, if he set them aside in one instance, he may be induced to repeat this act till his mind shall lose all confidence in itself, and become utterly debilitated. To this it may be added, that the critic ought never to forget that he is himself exposed to the same errors as the Poet, and, perhaps, in a much greater degree: for there can be no presumption in saying of most readers, that it is not probable they will be so well acquainted with the various stages of meaning through which words have passed, or with the fickleness or stability of the relations of particular ideas to each other; and, above all, since they are so much less interested in the subject, they may decide lightly and carelessly.

Long as the reader has been detained, I hope he will permit me to caution him against a mode of false criticism which has been applied to poetry, in which the language closely resembles that of life and nature. Such verses have been triumphed over in parodies, of which Dr. Johnson's stanza is a fair specimen: —

> "I put my hat upon my head
> And walked into the Strand,
> And there I met another man
> Whose hat was in his hand."

Immediately under these lines let us place one of the most justly-admired stanzas of the "Babes in the Wood."

PREFACE

"These pretty Babes with hand in hand
　　Went wandering up and down;
　　But never more they saw the Man
　　Approaching from the Town."

In both these stanzas the words, and the order of the words, in no respect differ from the most unimpassioned conversation. There are words in both, for example, "the Strand," and "the Town," connected with none but the most familiar ideas; yet the one stanza we admit as admirable, and the other as a fair example of the superlatively contemptible. Whence arises this difference? Not from the metre, not from the language, not from the order of the words; but the *matter* expressed in Dr. Johnson's stanza is contemptible. The proper method of treating trivial and simple verses, to which Dr. Johnson's stanza would be a fair parallelism, is not to say, this is a bad kind of poetry, or, this is not poetry; but, this wants sense; it is neither interesting in itself, nor can *lead* to anything interesting; the images neither originate in that sane state of feeling which arises out of thought, nor can excite thought or feeling in the Reader. This is the only sensible manner of dealing with such verses. Why trouble yourself about the species till you have previously decided upon the genus? Why take pains to prove that an ape is not a Newton, when it is self-evident that he is not a man?

One request I must make of my Reader, which is, that in judging these Poems he would decide by his own feelings genuinely, and not by reflection upon what will probably be the judgment of others. How common is it to hear a person say, I myself do not object to this style of composition, or this or that expression, but to such and such classes of people it will appear mean or ludicrous! This mode of criticism, so destructive of all sound unadulterated judgment, is almost universal: let the Reader then abide, independently, by his own feelings, and, if he finds himself affected, let him not suffer such conjectures to interfere with his pleasure.

If an Author, by any single composition, has impressed us with respect for his talents, it is useful to consider this as affording a presumption that on other occasions where we have been displeased he, nevertheless, may not have written ill or absurdly; and further, to give him so much credit for this one composition as may induce us to review what has displeased us with more care than we should otherwise have bestowed upon it. This is not only an act of justice, but, in our decisions upon poetry especially, may conduce, in a high degree, to the improvement of our own taste: for an *accurate* taste in poetry, and in all the other arts, as Sir Joshua Reynolds has observed, is an *acquired* talent, which can only be produced by thought and a long-continued intercourse with the best models of composition. This is mentioned, not with so ridiculous a purpose as to prevent the most inexperienced Reader from judging for himself (I have already said that I wish him to judge for himself), but merely to temper the rashness of decision, and to suggest that, if Poetry be a subject on which much time has not been bestowed, the judgment may be erroneous; and that, in many cases, it necessarily will be so.

Nothing would, I know, have so effectually contributed to further the end which I have in view, as to have shown of what kind the pleasure is, and how that pleasure is produced, which is confessedly produced by metrical composition essentially different from that which I have here endeavoured to recommend: for the Reader will say that he has been pleased by such composition; and what more can be done for him? The power of any art is limited; and he will suspect that, if it be proposed to furnish him with new friends, that can be only upon condition of his abandoning his old friends. Besides, as I have said, the Reader is himself conscious of the pleasure which he has received from such composition, composition to which he has peculiarly attached the endearing name of Poetry; and all men feel an habitual gratitude, and something of an honourable bigotry, for the objects which have long continued to please them: we not only wish to be pleased, but to be pleased in that particular way in which we have been accustomed to be pleased. There is in these feelings enough to resist a host of arguments; and I should be the less able to combat them successfully, as I am willing to allow that, in order entirely to enjoy the Poetry which I am recommending, it would be necessary to give up much of what is ordinarily enjoyed. But would my limits have permitted me to point out how this pleasure is produced, many obstacles might have been removed, and the Reader assisted in perceiving that the powers of language are not so limited as he may suppose; and that it is possible for poetry to give other enjoyments, of a purer, more lasting, and more exquisite nature. This part of the subject has not been altogether neglected, but it has not been so much my present aim to prove, that the interest excited by some other kinds of poetry is less vivid, and less worthy of the nobler powers of the mind, as to offer reasons for presuming that if my purpose were fulfilled, a species of poetry would be produced which is genuine poetry; in its nature well adapted to interest mankind permanently, and likewise important in the multiplicity and quality of its moral relations.

From what has been said, and from a perusal of the Poems, the Reader will be able to clearly perceive the object which I had in view: he will determine how far it has been attained, and, what is a much more important question, whether it be worth attaining: and upon the decision of these two questions will rest my claim to the approbation of the Public.

APPENDIX

1802

See page 27 — "by what is usually called POETIC DICTION."

PERHAPS, as I have no right to expect that attentive perusal, without which, confined, as I have been, to the narrow limits of a preface, my meaning cannot be thoroughly understood, I am anxious to give an exact notion of the sense in which the phrase poetic diction has been used; and for this purpose, a few words shall here be added, concerning the origin and characteristics of the phraseology which I have condemned under that name.

The earliest poets of all nations generally wrote from passion excited by real events; they wrote naturally, and as men: feeling powerfully as they did, their language was daring, and figurative. In succeeding times, Poets, and Men ambitious of the fame of Poets, perceiving the influence of such language, and desirous of producing the same effect without being animated by the same passion, set themselves to a mechanical adoption of these figures of speech, and made use of them, sometimes with propriety, but much more frequently applied them to feelings and thoughts with which they had no natural connections whatsoever. A language was thus insensibly produced, differing materially from the real language of men in *any situa-*

[39]

tion. The Reader or Hearer of this distorted language found himself in a perturbed and unusual state of mind: when affected by the genuine language of passion he had been in a perturbed and unusual state of mind also: in both cases he was willing that his common judgment and understanding should be laid asleep, and he had no instinctive and infallible perception of the true to make him reject the false; the one served as a passport for the other. The emotion was in both cases delightful, and no wonder if he confounded the one with the other, and believed them both to be produced by the same or similar causes. Besides, the Poet spake to him in the character of a man to be looked up to, a man of genius and authority. Thus, and from a variety of other causes, this distorted language was received with admiration; and Poets, it is probable, who had before contented themselves for the most part with misapplying only expressions which at first had been dictated by real passion, carried the abuse still further, and introduced phrases composed apparently in the spirit of the original figurative language of passion, yet altogether of their own invention, and characterised by various degrees of wanton deviation from good sense and nature.

It is indeed true that the language of the earliest Poets was felt to differ materially from ordinary language, because it was the language of extraordinary occasions; but it was really spoken by men, language which the Poet himself had uttered when he had been affected by the events which he described, or which he had heard uttered by those around him. To this language it is probable that metre of some sort or other was early superadded. This separated the genuine language of Poetry still further from common life, so that whoever read or heard the poems of these earliest Poets felt himself moved in a way in which he had not been accustomed to be moved in real life, and by causes manifestly different from those which acted upon him in real life. This was the great temptation to all the corruptions which have followed: under the protection of this feeling succeeding Poets constructed a phraseology which had one thing, it is true, in common with the genuine language of poetry, namely, that it was not heard in ordinary conversation; that it was unusual. But the first Poets, as I have said, spake a language which, though unusual, was still the language of men. This circumstance, however, was disregarded by their successors; they found that they could please by easier means: they became proud of modes of expression which they themselves had invented, and which were uttered only by themselves. In process of time metre became a symbol or promise of this unusual language, and whoever took upon him to write in metre, according as he possessed more or less of true poetic genius, introduced less or more of this adulterated phraseology into his compositions, and the true and the false were inseparably interwoven until, the taste of men becoming gradually perverted, this language was received as a natural language, and at length, by the influence of books upon men, did to a certain degree really become so. Abuses of this kind were imported from one nation to another, and with the progress of refinement this diction became daily more and more corrupt, thrusting out of sight the plain humanities of nature by a motley masquerade of tricks, quaintnesses, hieroglyphics, and enigmas.

It would not be uninteresting to point out the causes of the pleasure given by this extravagant and absurd diction. It depends upon a great variety of causes, but upon none, perhaps, more than its influence in impressing a notion of the peculiarity and exaltation of the Poet's character, and in flattering the Reader's self-love by bringing him nearer to a sympathy with that character; an effect which is accomplished by unsettling ordinary habits of thinking, and thus assisting the Reader to approach to that perturbed and dizzy state of mind in which if he does not find himself, he imagines that he is *balked* of a peculiar enjoyment which poetry can and ought to bestow.

The sonnet quoted from Gray in the Preface, except the lines printed in Italics, consists of little else but this diction, though not of the worst kind; and indeed, if one may be permitted to say so, it is far too common in the best writers, both ancient and modern. Perhaps in no way, by positive example, could more easily be given a notion of what I mean by the phrase *poetic diction* than by referring to a comparison between the metrical paraphrase which we have of passages in the Old and

New Testament, and those passages as they exist in our common Translation. See Pope's "Messiah" throughout; Prior's "Did sweeter sounds adorn my flowing tongue," etc. "Though I speak with the tongues of men and of angels," etc. 1st Corinthians, chap. xiii. By way of immediate example, take the following of Dr. Johnson: —

> "Turn on the prudent Ant thy heedless eyes,
> Observe her labours, Sluggard, and be wise;
> No stern command, no monitory voice,
> Prescribes her duties, or directs her choice;
> Yet, timely provident, she hastes away
> To snatch the blessings of a plenteous day;
> When fruitful Summer loads the teeming plain,
> She crops the harvest, and she stores the grain.
> How long shall sloth usurp thy useless hours,
> Unnerve thy vigour, and enchain thy powers?
> While artful shades thy downy couch enclose,
> And soft solicitation courts repose,
> Amidst the drowsy charms of dull delight,
> Year chases year with unremitted flight,
> Till Want now following, fraudulent and slow,
> Shall spring to seize thee, like an ambush'd foe."

From this hubbub of words pass to the original. "Go to the ant, thou sluggard; consider her ways, and be wise: which having no guide, overseer, or ruler, provideth her meat in the summer, and gathereth her food in the harvest. How long wilt thou sleep, O sluggard? when wilt thou arise out of thy sleep? Yet a little sleep, a little slumber, a little folding of the hands to sleep: so shall thy poverty come as one that travelleth, and thy want as an armed man." Proverbs, chap. vi.

One more quotation, and I have done. It is from Cowper's Verses supposed to be written by Alexander Selkirk: —

> "Religion! what treasure untold
> Resides in that heavenly word!
> More precious than silver and gold,
> Or all that this earth can afford.
> But the sound of the church-going bell
> These valleys and rocks never heard,
> Ne'er sighed at the sound of a knell,
> Or smiled when a sabbath appeared.
>
> Ye winds, that have made me your sport,
> Convey to this desolate shore
> Some cordial endearing report
> Of a land I must visit no more.
> My Friends, do they now and then send
> A wish or a thought after me?
> O tell me I yet have a friend,
> Though a friend I am never to see."

This passage is quoted as an instance of three different styles of composition. The first four lines are poorly expressed; some Critics would call the language prosaic; the fact is, it would be bad prose, so bad, that it is scarcely worse in metre. The epithet "church-going" applied to a bell, and that by so chaste a writer as Cowper, is an instance of the strange abuses which Poets have introduced into their language, till they and their Readers take them as matters of course, if they do not single them out expressly as objects of admiration. The two lines "Ne'er sighed at the sound," etc., are, in my opinion, an instance of the language of passion wrested from its proper use, and, from the mere circumstance of the composition being in metre, applied upon an occasion that does not justify such violent expressions; and I should condemn the passage, though perhaps few Readers will agree with me, as vicious poetic diction. The last stanza is throughout admirably expressed: it would be equally good whether in prose or verse, except that the Reader has an exquisite pleasure in seeing such natural language so naturally connected with metre. The beauty of this stanza tempts me to conclude with a principle which ought never to be lost sight of, and which has been my chief guide in all I have said, — namely, that in works *of imagination and sentiment*, for of these only have I been treating, in proportion as ideas and feelings are valuable, whether the composition be in prose or in verse, they require and exact one and the same language. Metre is but adventitious to composition, and the phraseology for which that passport is necessary, even where it may be graceful at all, will be little valued by the judicious.

DEDICATION

PREFIXED TO THE EDITION OF 1815

TO

SIR GEORGE HOWLAND BEAUMONT, BART.'

My dear Sir George,

Accept my thanks for the permission given me to dedicate these Volumes to you. In addition to a lively pleasure derived from general considerations, I feel a particular satisfaction; for, by inscribing these Poems with your Name, I seem to myself in some degree to repay, by an appropriate honour, the great obligation which I owe to one part of the Collection — as having been the means of first making us personally known to each other. Upon much of the remainder, also, you have a peculiar claim, — for some of the best pieces were composed under the shade of your own groves, upon the classic ground of Coleorton; where I was animated by the recollection of those illustrious Poets of your name and family, who were born in that neighbourhood; and, we may be assured, did not wander with indifference by the dashing stream of Grace Dieu, and among the rocks that diversify the forest of Charnwood. — Nor is there any one to whom such parts of this Collection as have been inspired or coloured by the beautiful Country from which I now address you, could be pre-

Rydal Mount

sented with more propriety than to yourself — to whom it has suggested so many admirable pictures. Early in life, the sublimity and beauty of this region excited your admiration; and I know that you are bound to it in mind by a still strengthening attachment.

Wishing and hoping that this Work, with the embellishments it has received from your pencil, may survive as a lasting memorial of a friendship, which I reckon among the blessings of my life,

I have the honour to be,

My dear Sir George,

Yours most affectionately and faithfully,

WILLIAM WORDSWORTH.

RYDAL MOUNT, WESTMORELAND,
February 1, 1815.

PREFACE TO THE EDITION OF 1815

THE powers requisite for the production of poetry are: first, those of Observation and Description, — *i. e.* the ability to observe with accuracy things as they are in themselves, and with fidelity to describe them, unmodified by any passion or feeling existing in the mind of the describer: whether the things depicted be actually present to the senses, or have a place only in the memory. This power, though indispensable to a Poet, is one which he employs only in submission to necessity, and never for a continuance of time: as its exercise supposes all the higher qualities of the mind to be passive, and in a state of subjection to external objects, much in the same way as a translator or engraver ought to be to his original. 2dly, Sensibility, — which the more exquisite it is, the wider will be the range of a poet's perceptions; and the more will he be incited to observe objects, both as they exist in themselves and as re-acted upon by his own mind. (The distinction between poetic and human sensibility has been marked in the character of the Poet delineated in the original preface.) 3dly, Reflection, — which makes the Poet acquainted with the value of actions, images, thoughts, and feelings; and assists the sensibility in perceiving their connection with each other. 4thly, Imagination and Fancy, — to modify, to create, and to associate.

[48]

5thly, Invention, — by which characters are composed out of materials supplied by observation; whether of the Poet's own heart and mind, or of external life and nature; and such incidents and situations produced as are most impressive to the imagination, and most fitted to do justice to the characters, sentiments, and passions, which the poet undertakes to illustrate. And, lastly, Judgment, — to decide how and where, and in what degree, each of these faculties ought to be exerted; so that the less shall not be sacrificed to the greater; nor the greater, slighting the less, arrogate, to its own injury, more than its due. By judgment, also, is determined what are the laws and appropriate graces of every species of composition.[1]

The materials of Poetry, by these powers collected and produced, are cast, by means of various moulds, into divers forms. The moulds may be enumerated, and the forms specified, in the following order. 1st, The Narrative, — including the Epopœia, the Historic Poem, the Tale, the Romance, the Mock-heroic, and, if the spirit of Homer will tolerate such neighbourhood, that dear production of our days, the metrical Novel. Of this Class, the distinguishing mark is, that the Narrator, however liberally his speaking agents be introduced, is himself the source from which everything primarily flows. Epic Poets, in order that their

[1] As sensibility to harmony of numbers, and the power of producing it, are invariably attendants upon the faculties above specified, nothing has been said upon those requisites.

[49]

mode of composition may accord with the elevation of their subject, represent themselves as *singing* from the inspiration of the Muse, "Arma virumque *cano*"; but this is a fiction, in modern times, of slight value, the "Iliad" or the "Paradise Lost" would gain little in our estimation by being chanted. The other poets who belong to this class are commonly content to *tell* their tale; — so that of the whole it may be affirmed that they neither require nor reject the accompaniment of music.

2dly, The Dramatic, — consisting of Tragedy, Historic Drama, Comedy, and Masque, in which the poet does not appear at all in his own person, and where the whole action is carried on by speech and dialogue of the agents; music being admitted only incidentally and rarely. The Opera may be placed here, inasmuch as it proceeds by dialogue; though depending, to the degree that it does, upon music, it has a strong claim to be ranked with the lyrical. The characteristic and impassioned Epistle, of which Ovid and Pope have given examples, considered as a species of monodrama, may, without impropriety, be placed in this class.

3dly, The Lyrical — containing the Hymn, the Ode, the Elegy, the Song, and the Ballad; in all which, for the production of their *full* effect, an accompaniment of music is indispensable.

4thly, The Idyllium, — descriptive chiefly either of the processes and appearances of external nature, as the "Seasons" of Thomson; or of characters, manners, and sentiments, as are Shenstone's "Schoolmistress," "The Cotter's Saturday Night" of Burns, the "Twa Dogs" of the same Author; or of these in conjunction with the appearances of Nature, as most of the pieces of Theocritus, the "Allegro" and "Penseroso" of Milton, Beattie's "Minstrel," Goldsmith's "Deserted Village." The Epitaph, the Inscription, the Sonnet, most of the epistles of poets writing in their own persons, and all loco-descriptive poetry, belong to this class.

5thly, Didactic, — the principal object of which is direct instruction; as the Poem of Lucretius, the "Georgics" of Virgil, "The Fleece," of Dyer, Mason's "English Garden," etc.

And, lastly, philosophical Satire, like that of Horace and Juvenal; personal and occasional Satire rarely comprehending sufficient of the general in the individual to be dignified with the name of poetry.

Out of the three last has been constructed a composite order, of which Young's "Night Thoughts," and Cowper's "Task," are excellent examples.

It is deducible from the above, that poems, apparently miscellaneous, may with propriety be arranged either with reference to the powers of mind *predominant* in the production of them; or to the mould in which they are cast; or lastly, to the subjects to which they relate. From each of these considerations, the following Poems have been divided into classes; which, that the work may more obviously correspond with the course of human life, and for the sake of exhibiting in it the three requisites of a legitimate whole, a beginning, a middle, and an end, have been also arranged, as far as it was possible, according to an order of time, commencing with Childhood, and terminating with Old Age, Death, and Immortality. My guiding wish was that the small pieces of which these volumes consist, thus discriminated, might be regarded under a two-fold view; as composing an entire work within themselves, and as adjuncts to the philosophical Poem, "The Recluse." This arrangement has long presented itself habitually to my own mind. Nevertheless, I should have preferred to scatter the contents of these volumes at random, if I had been persuaded that, by the plan adopted, anything material would be taken from the natural effect of the pieces, individually, on the mind of the unreflecting Reader. I trust there is a sufficient variety in each class to prevent this; while, for him who reads with reflection, the arrangement will serve as a commentary unostentatiously directing his attention to my purposes, both particular and general. But as I wish to guard against the possibility of misleading by this classification, it is proper first to remind the Reader that certain poems are placed according to the powers of mind, in the Author's conception, predominant in the production of them; *predominant*, which implies the exertion of other faculties in less degree. Where there is more imagination than fancy in a poem, it is placed under the head of imagination, and *vice versâ*.

PREFACE TO THE EDITION OF 1815

Both the above classes might without impropriety have been enlarged from that consisting of "Poems founded on the Affections"; as might this latter from those, and from the class "proceeding from Sentiment and Reflection." The most striking characteristics of each piece, mutual illustration, variety, and proportion, have governed me throughout.

None of the other Classes, except those of Fancy and Imagination, require any particular notice. But a remark of general application may be made. All Poets, except the dramatic, have been in the practice of feigning that their works were composed to the music of the harp or lyre: with what degree of affectation this has been done in modern times, I leave to the judicious to determine. For my own part, I have not been disposed to violate probability so far, or to make such a large demand upon the Reader's charity. Some of these pieces are essentially lyrical; and, therefore, cannot have their due force without a supposed musical accompaniment; but, in much the greatest part, as a substitute for the classic lyre or romantic harp, I require nothing more than an animated or impassioned recitation, adapted to the subject. Poems, however humble in their kind, if they be good in that kind, cannot read themselves; the law of long syllable and short must not be so inflexible, — the letter of metre must not be so impassive to the spirit of versification, — as to deprive the Reader of all voluntary power to modulate, in subordination to the sense, the music of the poem; — in the same manner as his mind is left at liberty, and even summoned, to act upon its thoughts and images. But, though the accompaniment of a musical instrument be frequently dispensed with, the true Poet does not therefore abandon his privilege distinct from that of the mere Proseman;

> "He murmurs near the running brooks
> A music sweeter than their own."

Let us come now to the consideration of the words Fancy and Imagination, as employed in the classification of the following Poems. "A man," says an intelligent author, "has imagination in proportion as he can distinctly copy in idea the impressions of sense: it is the faculty which *images* within the mind the phenomena of sensation. A man has fancy in proportion as he can call up, connect, or associate, at pleasure, those internal images ($\phi a \nu \tau \acute{a} \zeta \epsilon \iota \nu$ is to cause to appear), so as to complete ideal representations of absent objects. Imagination is the power of depicting, and fancy of evoking and combining. The imagination is formed by patient observation; the fancy by a voluntary activity in shifting the scenery of the mind. The more accurate the imagination, the more safely may a painter, or a poet, undertake a delineation, or a description, without the presence of the objects to be characterised. The more versatile the fancy, the more original and striking will be the decorations produced." — *British Synonyms discriminated, by W. Taylor.*

Is not this as if a man should undertake to supply an

[54]

account of a building, and be so intent upon what he had discovered of the foundation, as to conclude his task without once looking up at the superstructure? Here, as in other instances throughout the volume, the judicious Author's mind is enthralled by Etymology; he takes up the original word as his guide and escort and too often does not perceive how soon he becomes its prisoner, without liberty to tread in any path but that to which it confines him. It is not easy to find out how imagination, thus explained, differs from distinct remembrance of images; or fancy from quick and vivid recollection of them: each is nothing more than a mode of memory. If the two words bear the above meaning, and no other, what term is left to designate that faculty of which the Poet is "all compact"; he whose eye glances from earth to heaven, whose spiritual attributes body forth what his pen is prompt in turning to shape; or what is left to characterise Fancy, as insinuating herself into the heart of objects with creative activity? — Imagination, in the sense of the word as giving title to a class of the following Poems, has no reference to images that are merely a faithful copy, existing in the mind, of absent external objects; but is a word of higher import, denoting operations of the mind upon those objects, and processes of creation or of composition, governed by certain fixed laws. I proceed to illustrate my meaning by instances. A parrot *hangs* from the wires of his cage by his beak or by his claws; or a monkey from the bough of a tree by his paws or his tail. Each creature does so literally and actually. In the first Eclogue of Virgil, the shepherd, thinking of the time when he is to take leave of his farm, thus addresses his goats: —

> "Non ego vos posthac viridi projectus in antro
> Dumosa *pendere* procul de rupe videbo."

> —— "half way down
> *Hangs* one who gathers samphire,"

is the well-known expression of Shakespeare, delineating an ordinary image upon the cliffs of Dover. In these two instances is a slight exertion of the faculty which I denominate imagination, in the use of one word: neither the goats nor the samphire-gatherer do literally hang, as does the parrot or the monkey; but, presenting to the senses something of such an appearance, the mind in its activity, for its own gratification, contemplates them as hanging.

> "As when far off at sea a fleet descried
> *Hangs* in the clouds, by equinoctial winds
> Close sailing from Bengala, or the isles
> Of Ternate or Tidore, whence merchants bring
> Their spicy drugs; they on the trading flood
> Through the wide Ethiopian to the Cape
> Ply, stemming nightly toward the Pole: so seemed
> Far off the flying Fiend."

Here is the full strength of the imagination involved in the word *hangs*, and exerted upon the whole image: First, the fleet, an aggregate of many ships, is represented as one mighty person, whose track, we know and feel, is upon the waters; but, taking advantage of its appearance to the senses, the Poet dares to represent it as *hanging in the clouds*, both for the gratification of the mind in contemplating the image itself, and in reference to the motion and appearance of the sublime objects to which it is compared.

From impressions of sight we will pass to those of sound; which, as they must necessarily be of a less definite character, shall be selected from these volumes: —

"Over his own sweet voice the Stock-dove *broods*,"

of the same bird,

"His voice was *buried* among trees,
Yet to be come at by the breeze" ;

"O, Cuckoo! shall I call thee *Bird*,
Or but a wondering *Voice?*"

The stock-dove is said to *coo*, a sound well imitating the note of the bird; but, by the intervention of the metaphor *broods*, the affections are called in by the imagination to assist in marking the manner in which the bird reiterates and prolongs her soft note, as if herself delighting to listen to it, and participating of a still and quiet satisfaction, like that which may be supposed inseparable from the continuous process of incubation. "His voice was buried among trees," a metaphor expressing the love of *seclusion* by which this Bird is marked; and characterising its note as not partaking of the shrill and the piercing, and therefore more easily deadened by the intervening shade; yet a note so peculiar and withal so pleasing, that the breeze, gifted with that love of the sound which the Poet feels, penetrates the shades in which it is entombed, and conveys it to the ear of the listener.

> "Shall I call thee Bird,
> Or but a wandering Voice ?"

This concise interrogation characterises the seeming ubiquity of the voice of the cuckoo, and dispossesses the creature almost of a corporeal existence; the Imagination being tempted to this exertion of her power by a consciousness in the memory that the cuckoo is almost perpetually heard throughout the season of spring, but seldom becomes an object of sight.

Thus far of images independent of each other, and immediately endowed by the mind with properties that do not inhere in them, upon an incitement from properties and qualities the existence of which is inherent and obvious. These processes of imagination are carried on either by conferring additional properties upon an object, or abstracting from it some of those which it actually possesses, and thus enabling it to re-act upon the mind which hath performed the process like a new existence.

I pass from the Imagination acting upon an individual image to a consideration of the same faculty employed upon images in a conjunction by which they modify each other. The Reader has already had a fine instance before him in the passage quoted from

Virgil, where the apparently perilous situation of the goat, hanging upon the shaggy precipice, is contrasted with that of the shepherd contemplating it from the seclusion of the cavern in which he lies stretched at ease and in security. Take these images separately, and how unaffecting the picture compared with that produced by their being thus connected with, and opposed to, each other!

> "As a huge stone is sometimes seen to lie
> Couched on the bald top of an eminence,
> Wonder to all who do the same espy
> By what means it could thither come, and whence,
> So that it seems a thing endued with sense,
> Like a sea-beast crawled forth, which on a shelf
> Of rock or sand reposeth, there to sun himself.
>
> Such seemed this Man; not all alive or dead,
> Nor all asleep, in his extreme old age.
>
> . . . .
>
> Motionless as a cloud the old Man stood,
> That heareth not the loud winds when they call,
> And moveth altogether if it move at all."

In these images, the conferring, the abstracting, and the modifying powers of the Imagination, immediately and mediately acting, are all brought into conjunction. The stone is endowed with something of the power of life to approximate it to the sea-beast; and the sea-beast stripped of its vital qualities to assimilate it to the stone; which intermediate image is thus treated for the purpose of bringing the original image, that of the stone, to a nearer resemblance to the figure and condi-

tion of the aged Man; who is divested of so much of
the indications of life and motion as to bring him to the
point where the two objects unite and coalesce in just
comparison. After what has been said, the image of
the cloud need not be commented upon.

Thus far of an endowing or modifying power; but the
imagination also shapes and *creates;* and how? By innumerable processes; and in none does it more delight
than in that of consolidating numbers into unity, and
dissolving and separating unity into number, — alter-
nations proceeding from, and governed by, a sublime
consciousness of the soul in her own mighty and almost
divine powers. Recur to the passage already cited from
Milton. When the compact Fleet, as one Person, has
been introduced "Sailing from Bengala," "They,"
i. e. the "merchants," representing the fleet resolved
into a multitude of ships, "ply" their voyage towards
the extremities of the earth: "So" (referring to the
word "As" in the commencement) "seemed the fly-
ing Fiend"; the image of his Person acting to recom-
bine the multitude of ships into one body, — the point
from which the comparison set out. "So seemed," and
to whom seemed? To the heavenly Muse who dictates
the poem, to the eye of the Poet's mind, and to that
of the Reader, present at one moment in the wide
Ethiopian, and the next in the solitudes, then first
broken in upon, of the infernal regions!

"Modo me Thebis, modo ponit Athenis."

Hear again this mighty Poet, — speaking of the Messiah going forth to expel from heaven the rebellious angels,

> "Attended by ten thousand thousand Saints
> He onward came: far off his coming shone," —

the retinue of Saints, and the Person of the Messiah himself, lost almost and merged in the splendour of that indefinite abstraction "His coming"!

As I do not mean here to treat this subject further than to throw some light upon the present Volumes, and especially upon one division of them, I shall spare myself and the Reader the trouble of considering the Imagination as it deals with thoughts and sentiments, as it regulates the composition of characters, and determines the course of actions: I will not consider it (more than I have already done by implication) as that power which, in the language of one of my most esteemed Friends, "draws all things to one; which makes things animate or inanimate, beings with their attributes, subjects with their accessories, take one colour and serve to one effect." [1] The grand storehouses of enthusiastic and meditative Imagination, of poetical, as contradistinguished from human and dramatic Imagination, are the prophetic and lyrical parts of the Holy Scriptures, and the works of Milton; to which I cannot forbear to add those of Spenser. I select these writers in preference to those of ancient Greece and Rome, because the anthropomorphism of the Pagan religion

[1] Charles Lamb upon the genius of Hogarth.

subjected the minds of the greatest poets in those countries too much to the bondage of definite form; from
which the Hebrews were preserved by their abhorrence
of idolatry. This abhorrence was almost as strong in
our great epic Poet, both from circumstances of his life,
and from the constitution of his mind. However im-
bued the surface might be with classical literature, he
was a Hebrew in soul; and all things tended in him
towards the sublime. Spenser, of a gentler nature,
maintained his freedom by aid of his allegorical spirit,
at one time inciting him to create persons out of ab-
stractions; and, at another, by a superior effort of genius,
to give the universality and permanence of abstrac-
tions to his human beings, by means of attributes and
emblems that belong to the highest moral truths and
the purest sensations, — of which his character of Una
is a glorious example. Of the human and dramatic
Imagination the works of Shakspeare are an inex-
haustible source.

> "I tax not you, ye Elements, with unkindness,
> I never gave you kingdoms, call'd you Daughters!"

And if, bearing in mind the many Poets distinguished
by this prime quality, whose names I omit to mention,
yet justified by recollection of the insults which the
ignorant, the incapable, and the presumptuous, have
heaped upon these and my other writings, I may be
permitted to anticipate the judgment of posterity upon
myself, I shall declare (censurable, I grant, if the noto-
riety of the fact above stated does not justify me) that

I have given in these unfavourable times evidence of exertions of this faculty upon its worthiest objects, the external universe, the moral and religious sentiments of Man, his natural affections, and his acquired passions; which have the same ennobling tendency as the productions of men, in this kind, worthy to be holden in undying remembrance.

To the mode in which Fancy has already been characterized as the power of evoking and combining, or, as my friend Mr. Coleridge has styled it, "the aggregative and associative power," my objection is only that the definition is too general. To aggregate and to associate, to evoke and to combine, belong as well to the Imagination as to the Fancy; but either the materials evoked and combined are different, or they are brought together under a different law, and for a different purpose. Fancy does not require that the materials which she makes use of should be susceptible of change in their constitution from her touch; and, where they admit of modification, it is enough for her purpose if it be slight, limited, and evanescent. Directly the reverse of these are the desires and demands of the Imagination. She recoils from everything but the plastic, the pliant, and the indefinite. She leaves it to Fancy to describe Queen Mab as coming,

> "In shape no bigger than an agate-stone
> On the fore-finger of an alderman."

Having to speak of stature, she does not tell you that her gigantic Angel was as tall as Pompey's Pillar; much less that he was twelve cubits or twelve hundred cubits high; or that his dimensions equalled those of Teneriffe or Atlas; — because these, and if they were a million times as high it would be the same, are bounded: The expression is, "His stature reached the sky!" the illimitable firmament! — When the Imagination frames a comparison, if it does not strike on the first presentation, a sense of the truth of the likeness, from the moment that it is perceived, grows — and continues to grow — upon the mind; the resemblance depending less upon outline of form and feature than upon expression and effect; less upon casual and outstanding than upon inherent and internal properties: moreover, the images invariably modify each other. — The law under which the processes of Fancy are carried on is as capricious as the accidents of things, and the effects are surprising, playful, ludicrous, amusing, tender, or pathetic, as the objects happen to be appositely produced or fortunately combined. Fancy depends upon the rapidity and profusion with which she scatters her thoughts and images; trusting that their number, and the felicity with which they are linked together, will make amends for the want of individual value: or she prides herself upon the curious subtilty and the successful elaboration with which she can detect their lurking affinities. If she can win you over to her purpose, and impart to you her feelings, she cares not how unstable or transitory may be her influence, knowing that it will not be out of her power to resume it upon an apt occasion. But the Imagination

[64]

is conscious of an indestructible dominion; — the Soul may fall away from it, not being able to sustain its grandeur; but, if once felt and acknowledged, by no act of any other faculty of the mind can it be relaxed, impaired, or diminished. — Fancy is given to quicken and to beguile the temporal part of our nature, Imagination to incite and to support the eternal. — Yet it is not the less true that Fancy, as she is an active, is also, under her own laws and in her own spirit, a creative faculty. In what manner Fancy ambitiously aims at a rivalship with Imagination, and Imagination stoops to work with the materials of Fancy, might be illustrated from the compositions of all eloquent writers, whether in prose or verse; and chiefly from those of our own Country. Scarcely a page of the impassioned parts of Bishop Taylor's Works can be opened that shall not afford examples. — Referring the Reader to those inestimable volumes, I will content myself with placing a conceit (ascribed to Lord Chesterfield) in contrast with a passage from the " Paradise Lost": —

"The dews of the evening most carefully shun,
They are the tears of the sky for the loss of the sun."

After the transgression of Adam, Milton, with other appearances of sympathising Nature, thus marks the immediate consequence,

"Sky lowered, and, muttering thunder, some sad drops
Wept at completing of the mortal sin."

The associating link is the same in each instance: Dew and rain, not distinguishable from the liquid substance of tears, are employed as indications of sorrow. A flash of surprise is the effect in the former case; a flash of surprise, and nothing more; for the nature of things does not sustain the combination. In the latter, the effects from the act, of which there is this immediate consequence and visible sign, are so momentous that the mind acknowledges the justice and reasonableness of the sympathy in nature so manifested; and the sky weeps drops of water as if with human eyes, as "Earth had before trembled from her entrails, and Nature given a second groan."

Finally, I will refer to Cotton's "Ode upon Winter," an admirable composition, though stained with some peculiarities of the age in which he lived, for a general illustration of the characteristics of Fancy. The middle part of this ode contains a most lively description of the entrance of Winter, with his retinue, as "A palsied king," and yet a military monarch, — advancing for conquest with his army; the several bodies of which, and their arms and equipments, are described with a rapidity of detail, and a profusion of *fanciful* comparisons, which indicate on the part of the poet extreme activity of intellect, and a correspondent hurry of delightful feeling. Winter retires from the foe into his fortress, where

> —— "a magazine
> Of sovereign juice is cellared in;
> Liquor that will the seige maintain
> Should Phœbus ne'er return again."

PREFACE TO THE EDITION OF 1815

Though myself a water-drinker, I cannot resist the pleasure of transcribing what follows, as an instance still more happy of Fancy employed in the treatment of feeling than, in its preceding passages, the Poem supplies of her management of forms.

> "'T is that, that gives the poet rage,
> And thaws the gelly'd blood of age;
> Matures the young, restores the old,
> And makes the fainting coward bold.

> " It lays the careful head to rest,
> Calms palpitations in the breast,
> Renders our lives' misfortune sweet;
>
> .   .   .   .

> " Then let the chill Sirocco blow,
> And gird us round with hills of snow,
> Or else go whistle to the shore,
> And make the hollow mountains roar,

> " Whilst we together jovial sit
> Careless, and crowned with mirth and wit,
> Where, though bleak winds confine us home,
> Our fancies round the world shall roam.

> " We'll think of all the Friends we know,
> And drink to all worth drinking to;
> When having drunk all thine and mine,
> We rather shall want healths than wine.

> " But where Friends fail us, we'll supply
> Our friendships with our charity;
> Men that remote in sorrows live,
> Shall by our lusty brimmers thrive.

[67]

> " We'll drink the wanting into wealth,
>   And those that languish into health,
>   The afflicted into joy; th' opprest
>   Into security and rest.
>
> " The worthy in disgrace shall find
>   Favour return again more kind,
>   And in restraint who stifled lie,
>   Shall taste the air of liberty.
>
> " The brave shall triumph in success,
>   The lovers shall have mistresses,
>   Poor unregarded Virtue, praise,
>   And the neglected Poet, bays.
>
> " Thus shall our healths do others good,
>   Whilst we ourselves do all we would;
>   For, freed from envy and from care,
>   What would we be but what we are ? "

When I sate down to write this Preface, it was my intention to have made it more comprehensive; but, thinking that I ought rather to apologise for detaining the reader so long, I will here conclude.

ESSAY, SUPPLEMENTARY TO THE PREFACE

1815

WITH the young of both sexes, Poetry is like love, a passion; but, for much of the greater part of those who have been proud of its power over their minds, a necessity soon arises of breaking the pleasing bondage; or it relaxes of itself; — the thoughts being occupied in domestic cares, or the time engrossed by business. Poetry then becomes only an occasional recreation, while to those whose existence passes away in a course of fashionable pleasure, it is a species of luxurious amusement. In middle and declining age, a scattered number of serious persons resort to poetry, as to religion, for a protection against the pressure of trivial employments, and as a consolation for the afflictions of life. And, lastly, there are many who, having been enamoured of this art in their youth, have found leisure, after youth was spent, to cultivate general literature; in which poetry has continued to be comprehended *as a study*.

Into the above classes the Readers of poetry may be divided; Critics abound in them all; but from the last only can opinions be collected of absolute value, and worthy to be depended upon, as prophetic of the destiny of a new work. The young, who in nothing can

escape delusion, are especially subject to it in their intercourse with Poetry. The cause, not so obvious as the
fact is unquestionable, is the same as that from which
erroneous judgments in this art, in the minds of men of
all ages, chiefly proceed; but upon Youth it operates
with peculiar force. The appropriate business of poetry
(which, nevertheless, if genuine, is as permanent as
pure science), her appropriate employment, her privilege and her *duty*, is to treat of things not as they *are*,
but as they *appear;* not as they exist in themselves, but
as they *seem* to exist to the *senses*, and to the *passions*.
What a world of delusion does this acknowledged obligation prepare for the inexperienced! what temptations
to go astray are here held forth for them whose thoughts
have been little disciplined by the understanding, and
whose feelings revolt from the sway of reason! —
When a juvenile Reader is in the height of his rapture
with some vicious passage, should experience throw in
doubts, or common sense suggest suspicions, a lurking
consciousness that the realities of the Muse are but shows,
and that her liveliest excitements are raised by tran-
sient shocks of conflicting feeling and successive assem-
blages of contradictory thoughts — is ever at hand to
justify extravagance, and to sanction absurdity. But,
it may be asked, as these illusions are unavoidable, and,
no doubt, eminently useful to the mind as a process,
what good can be gained by making observations, the
tendency of which is to diminish the confidence of youth
in its feelings, and thus to abridge its innocent and

even profitable pleasures? The reproach implied in the question could not be warded off, if Youth were incapable of being delighted with what is truly excellent; or if these errors always terminated of themselves in due season. But, with the majority, though their force be abated, they continue through life. Moreover, the fire of youth is too vivacious an element to be extinguished or damped by a philosophical remark; and, while there is no danger that what has been said will be injurious or painful to the ardent and the confident, it may prove beneficial to those who, being enthusiastic, are, at the same time, modest and ingenuous. The intimation may unite with their own misgivings to regulate their sensibility, and to bring in, sooner than it would otherwise have arrived, a more discreet and sound judgment.

If it should excite wonder that men of ability, in later life, whose understandings have been rendered acute by practice in affairs, should be so easily and so far imposed upon when they happen to take up a new work in verse, this appears to be the cause; — that, having discontinued their attention to poetry, whatever progress may have been made in other departments of knowledge, they have not, as to this art, advanced in true discernment beyond the age of youth. If, then, a new poem fall in their way, whose attractions are of that kind which would have enraptured them during the heat of youth, the judgment not being improved to a degree that they shall be disgusted, they are dazzled; and prize and cherish the faults for having had power to make the present time vanish before them, and to throw the mind back, as by enchantment, into the happiest season of life. As they read, powers seem to be revived, passions are regenerated, and pleasures restored. The Book was probably taken up after an escape from the burden of business, and with a wish to forget the world, and all its vexations and anxieties. Having obtained this wish, and so much more, it is natural that they should make report as they have felt.

If Men of mature age, through want of practice, be thus easily beguiled into admiration of absurdities, extravagances, and misplaced ornaments, thinking it proper that their understandings should enjoy a holiday, while they are unbending their minds with verse, it may be expected that such Readers will resemble their former selves also in strength of prejudice, and an inaptitude to be moved by the unostentatious beauties of a pure style. In the higher poetry, an enlightened Critic chiefly looks for a reflection of the wisdom of the heart and the grandeur of the imagination. Wherever these appear, simplicity accompanies them; Magnificence herself, when legitimate, depending upon a simplicity of her own, to regulate her ornaments. But it is a well-known property of human nature, that our estimates are ever governed by comparisons, of which we are conscious with various degrees of distinctness. Is it not, then, inevitable (confining these observations to the effects of style merely) that an eye, accustomed to the glaring hues of diction by which such Readers are caught and excited, will for the most part be rather repelled than attracted by an original Work, the colouring of which is disposed according to a pure and refined scheme of harmony? It is in the fine arts as in the affairs of life, no man can *serve* (*i. e.* obey with zeal and fidelity) two Masters.

As Poetry is most just to its own divine origin when it administers the comforts and breathes the spirit of religion, they who have learned to perceive this truth, and who betake themselves to reading verse for sacred purposes, must be preserved from numerous illusions to which the two Classes of Readers, whom we have been considering, are liable. But as the mind grows serious from the weight of life, the range of its passions is contracted accordingly; and its sympathies become so exclusive that many species of high excellence wholly escape, or but languidly excite, its notice. Besides, men who read from religious or moral inclinations, even when the subject is of that kind which they approve, are beset with misconceptions and mistakes peculiar to themselves. Attaching so much importance to the truths which interest them, they are prone to over-rate the Authors by whom those truths are expressed and enforced. They come prepared to impart so much passion to the Poet's language, that they remain unconscious how little, in fact, they received from it. And, on the other hand, religious faith is to him who holds it so momentous a thing, and error appears to be attended with such

tremendous consequences, that, if opinions touching upon religion occur which the Reader condemns, he not
only cannot sympathise with them, however animated
the expression, but there is, for the most part, an end
put to all satisfaction and enjoyment. Love, if it before
existed, is converted into dislike; and the heart of the
Reader is set against the Author and his book. — To
these excesses they, who from their professions ought to
be the most guarded against them, are perhaps the
most liable; I mean those sects whose religion, being
from the calculating understanding, is cold and formal.
For when Christianity, the religion of humility, is
founded upon the proudest faculty of our nature, what
can be expected but contradictions? Accordingly, be-
lievers of this cast are at one time contemptuous; at
another, being troubled, as they are and must be, with
inward misgivings, they are jealous and suspicious; and
at all seasons they are under temptation to supply, by
the heat with which they defend their tenets, the ani-
mation which is wanting to the constitution of the religion itself.

Faith was given to man that his affections, detached
from the treasures of time, might be inclined to settle
upon those of eternity: — the elevation of his nature,
which this habit produces on earth, being to him a pre-
sumptive evidence of a future state of existence, and
giving him a title to partake of its holiness. The religious man values what he sees chiefly as an "imperfect
shadowing forth" of what he is incapable of seeing. The

concerns of religion refer to indefinite objects, and are too weighty for the mind to support them without relieving itself by resting a great part of the burthen upon words and symbols. The commerce between Man and his Maker cannot be carried on but by a process where much is represented in little, and the Infinite Being accommodates himself to a finite capacity. In all this may be perceived the affinity between religion and poetry; between religion — making up the deficiencies of reason by faith; and poetry — passionate for the instruction of reason; between religion — whose element is infinitude, and whose ultimate trust is the supreme of things, submitting herself to circumscription, and reconciled to substitutions; and poetry — ethereal and transcendent, yet incapable to sustain her existence without sensuous incarnation. In this community of nature may be perceived also the lurking incitements of kindred error; — so that we shall find that no poetry has been more subject to distortion than that species, the argument and scope of which is religious; and no lovers of the art have gone farther astray than the pious and the devout.

Whither then shall we turn for that union of qualifications which must necessarily exist before the decisions of a critic can be of absolute value? For a mind at once poetical and philosophical; for a critic whose affections are as free and kindly as the spirit of society, and whose understanding is severe as that of dispassionate government? Where are we to look for that initiatory composure of mind which no selfishness can disturb? For a natural sensibility that has been tutored into correctness without losing anything of its quickness; and for active faculties, capable of answering the demands which an Author of original imagination shall make upon them, associated with a judgment that cannot be duped into admiration by aught that is unworthy of it? — among those and those only, who, never having suffered their youthful love of poetry to remit much of its force, have applied to the consideration of the laws of this art the best power of their understandings. At the same time it must be observed that, as this Class comprehends the only judgments which are trustworthy, so does it include the most erroneous and perverse. For to be mistaught is worse than to be untaught; and no perverseness equals that which is supported by system, no errors are so difficult to root out as those which the understanding has pledged its credit to uphold. In this Class are contained censors, who, if they be pleased with what is good, are pleased with it only by imperfect glimpses, and upon false principles; who, should they generalise rightly to a certain point, are sure to suffer for it in the end; who, if they stumble upon a sound rule, are fettered by misapplying it, or by straining it too far; being incapable of perceiving when it ought to yield to one of higher order. In it are found critics too petulant to be passive to a genuine poet, and too feeble to grapple with him; men, who take upon them to report of the course which *he* holds whom they are utterly unable to accompany, — confounded if he turn quick upon the wing, dismayed if he soar steadily "into the region"; — men of palsied imaginations and indurated hearts; in whose minds all healthy action is languid, who therefore feed as the many direct them, or, with the many, are greedy after vicious provocatives; — judges, whose censure is auspicious, and whose praise ominous! In this class meet together the two extremes of best and worst!

The observations presented in the foregoing series are of too ungracious a nature to have been made without reluctance; and, were it only on this account, I would invite the reader to try them by the test of comprehensive experience. If the number of judges who can be confidently relied upon be in reality so small, it ought to follow that partial notice only, or neglect, perhaps long continued, or attention wholly inadequate to their merits, must have been the fate of most works in the higher departments of poetry; and that, on the other hand, numerous productions have blazed into popularity, and have passed away, leaving scarcely a trace behind them: it will be further found, that when Authors shall have at length raised themselves into general admiration and maintained their ground, errors and prejudices have prevailed concerning their genius and their works, which the few who are conscious of those errors and prejudices would deplore; if they were not recompensed by perceiving that there are select Spirits for whom it is ordained that their fame shall be in the world an existence like that of Virtue, which owes its being to the struggles it makes, and its vigour to the enemies whom it provokes; — a vivacious quality, ever doomed to meet with opposition, and still triumphing over it; and, from the nature of its dominion, incapable of being brought to the sad conclusion of Alexander, when he wept that there were no more worlds for him to conquer.

Let us take a hasty retrospect of the poetical literature of this Country for the greater part of the last two centuries, and see if the facts support these inferences.

Who is there that now reads the "Creation" of Dubartas? Yet all Europe once resounded with his praise; he was caressed by kings; and, when his Poem was translated into our language, the "Faery Queen" faded before it. The name of Spenser, whose genius is of a higher order than even that of Ariosto, is at this day scarcely known beyond the limits of the British Isles. And if the value of his works is to be estimated from the attention now paid to them by his countrymen, compared with that which they bestow on those of some other writers, it must be pronounced small indeed.

> "The laurel, meed of mighty conquerors
> And poets *sage*" —

are his own words; but his wisdom has, in this particular, been his worst enemy: while its opposite, whether in the shape of folly or madness, has been *their* best friend. But he was a great power, and bears a high name: the laurel has been awarded to him.

A dramatic Author, if he write for the stage, must adapt himself to the taste of the audience, or they will not endure him; accordingly the mighty genius of Shakspeare was listened to. The people were delighted, but I am not sufficiently versed in stage antiquities to determine whether they did not flock as eagerly to the representation of many pieces of contemporary Authors, wholly undeserving to appear upon the same boards. Had there been a formal contest for superiority among dramatic writers, that Shakspeare, like his predecessors Sophocles and Euripides, would have often been subject to the mortification of seeing the prize adjudged to sorry competitors, becomes too probable, when we reflect that the admirers of Settle and Shadwell were, in a later age, as numerous, and reckoned as respectable in point of talent, as those of Dryden. At all events, that Shakspeare stooped to accommodate himself to the People, is sufficiently apparent; and one of the most striking proofs of his almost omnipotent genius is, that he could turn to such glorious purpose those materials which the prepossessions of the age compelled him to make use of. Yet even this marvellous skill appears not to have been enough to prevent his rivals from having some advantage over him in public estimation; else how can we account for passages and scenes that exist in his works, unless upon a supposition that some of the grossest of them, a fact which in my own mind I have no doubt of, were foisted in by the Players, for the gratification of the many?

But that his Works, whatever might be their reception upon the stage, made but little impression upon the ruling Intellects of the time, may be inferred from the fact that Lord Bacon, in his multifarious writings, nowhere either quotes or alludes to him.[1] — His dramatic excellence enabled him to resume possession of the stage after the Restoration; but Dryden tells us that in his time two of the plays of Beaumont and Fletcher were acted for one of Shakspeare's. And so faint and limited was the perception of the poetic beauties of his dramas in the time of Pope, that, in his Edition of the Plays, with a view of rendering to the general reader a necessary service, he printed between inverted commas those passages which he thought most worthy of notice.

At this day, the French Critics have abated nothing of their aversion to this darling of our Nation: "the English, with their bouffon de Shakspeare," is as familiar an expression among them as in the time of Voltaire. Baron Grimm is the only French writer who seems to have perceived his infinite superiority to the first names of the French Theatre; an advantage which the Parisian critic owed to his German blood and German education. The most enlightened Italians, though well acquainted with our language, are wholly incompetent to measure the proportions of Shakspeare.

[1] The learned Hakewill (a third edition of whose book bears date 1635), writing to refute the error "touching Nature's perpetual and universal decay," cites triumphantly the names of Ariosto, Tasso, Bartas, and Spenser, as instances that poetic genius had not degenerated; but he makes no mention of Shakspeare.

ESSAY, SUPPLEMENTARY TO THE PREFACE

The Germans only, of foreign nations, are approaching towards a knowledge and feeling of what he is. In some respects they have acquired a superiority over the fellow-countrymen of the Poet: for among us it is a current, I might say an established opinion, that Shakspeare is justly praised when he is pronounced to be "a wild irregular genius, in whom great faults are compensated by great beauties." How long may it be before this misconception passes away, and it becomes universally acknowledged that the judgment of Shakspeare in the selection of his materials, and in the manner in which he has made them, heterogeneous as they often are, constitute a unity of their own, and contribute all to one great end, is not less admirable than his imagination, his invention, and his intuitive knowledge of human Nature!

There is extant a small volume of miscellaneous poems, in which Shakspeare expresses his own feelings in his own person. It is not difficult to conceive that the Editor, George Steevens, should have been insensible to the beauties of one portion of that Volume, the Sonnets; though in no part of the writings of this Poet is found, in an equal compass, a greater number of exquisite feelings felicitously expressed. But, from regard to the Critic's own credit, he would not have ventured to talk of an [1] act of parliament not being strong enough

[1] This flippant insensibility was publicly reprehended by Mr. Coleridge in a course of Lectures upon Poetry given by him at the Royal Institution. For the various merits of thought and language

to compel the perusal of those little pieces, if he had not known that the people of England were ignorant of the treasures contained in them: and if he had not, more-over, shared the too common propensity of human nature to exult over a supposed fall into the mire of a genius whom he had been compelled to regard with ad-miration, as an inmate of the celestial regions — "there sitting where he durst not soar."

Nine years before the death of Shakspeare, Milton was born; and early in life he published several small poems, which, though on their first appearance they were praised by a few of the judicious, were afterwards neglected to that degree, that Pope in his youth could borrow from them without risk of its being known. Whether these poems are at this day justly appreciated, I will not undertake to decide: nor would it imply a severe reflection upon the mass of readers to suppose the contrary; seeing that a man of the acknowledged genius of Voss, the German poet, could suffer their spirit to evaporate; and could change their character, as is done in the translation made by him of the most popular of those pieces. At all events, it is certain that these Poems of Milton are now much read, and loudly praised; yet were they little heard of till more than 150 years after their publication; and of the Sonnets, Dr. Johnson, as appears from Boswell's Life of him, was in

in Shakspeare's Sonnets see Numbers 27, 29, 30, 32, 33, 54, 64, 66, 68, 73, 76, 86, 91, 92, 93, 97, 98, 105, 107, 108, 109, 111, 113, 114, 116, 117, 129, and many others.

the habit of thinking and speaking as contemptuously as Steevens wrote upon those of Shakspeare.

About the time when the Pindaric odes of Cowley and his imitators, and the productions of that class of curious thinkers whom Dr. Johnson has strangely styled metaphysical Poets, were beginning to lose something of that extravagant admiration which they had excited, the "Paradise Lost" made its appearance. "Fit audience find though few," was the petition addressed by the Poet to his inspiring Muse. I have said elsewhere that he gained more than he asked; this I believe to be true; but Dr. Johnson has fallen into a gross mistake when he attempts to prove, by the sale of the work, that Milton's Countrymen were "*just* to it" upon its first appearance. Thirteen hundred Copies were sold in two years; an uncommom example, he asserts, of the prevalence of genius in opposition to so much recent enmity as Milton's public conduct had excited. But, be it remembered that, if Milton's political and religious opinions, and the manner in which he announced them, had raised him many enemies, they had procured him numerous friends; who, as all personal danger was passed away at the time of publication, would be eager to procure the master-work of a man whom they revered, and whom they would be proud of praising. Take, from the number of purchasers, persons of this class, and also those who wished to possess the Poem as a religious work, and but few, I fear, would be left who sought for it on account of its poetical merits.

The demand did not immediately increase; "for," says Dr. Johnson, "many more readers" (he means persons in the habit of reading poetry) "than were supplied at first the Nation did not afford." How careless must a writer be who can make this assertion in the face of so many existing title-pages to belie it! Turning to my own shelves, I find the folio of Cowley, seventh edition, 1681. A book near it is Flatman's Poems, fourth edition, 1686; Waller, fifth edition, same date. The Poems of Norris of Bemerton not long after went, I believe, through nine editions. What further demand there might be for these works I do not know; but I well remember that, twenty-five years ago, the booksellers' stalls in London swarmed with the folios of Cowley. This is not mentioned in disparagement of that able writer and amiable man; but merely to show that, if Milton's work were not more read, it was not because readers did nor exist at the time. The early editions of the "Paradise Lost" were printed in a shape which allowed them to be sold at a low price, yet only three thousand copies of the Work were sold in eleven years; and the Nation, says Dr. Johnson, had been satisfied from 1623 to 1664, that is, forty-one years, with only two editions of the Works of Shakspeare, which probably did not together make one thousand Copies; facts adduced by the critic to prove the "paucity of Readers." — There were readers in multitudes; but their money went for other purposes, as their admiration was fixed elsewhere. We are authorized, then, to affirm that the reception of the "Paradise Lost," and the slow progress of its fame, are proofs as striking as can be desired that the positions which I am attempting to establish are not erroneous.[1] — How amusing to shape to one's self such a critique as a Wit of Charles's days, or a Lord of the Miscellanies or trading Journalist of King William's time, would have brought forth, if he had set his faculties industriously to work upon this Poem, everywhere impregnated with *original* excellence.

So strange indeed are the obliquities of admiration, that they whose opinions are much influenced by authority will often be tempted to think that there are no fixed principles [2] in human nature for this art to rest upon. I have been honoured by being permitted to peruse in MS. a tract composed between the period of the Revolution and the close of that century. It is the Work of an English Peer of high accomplishments, its object to form the character and direct the studies of his son. Perhaps nowhere does a more beautiful treatise of the kind exist. The good sense and wisdom of the thoughts, the delicacy of the feelings, and the charm of the style, are throughout equally conspicuous. Yet the Author, selecting among the Poets of his own country those

[1] Hughes is express upon this subject: in his dedication of Spenser's Works to Lord Somers, he writes thus: "It was your Lordship's encouraging a beautiful Edition of 'Paradise Lost' that first brought that incomparable Poem to be generally known and esteemed."

[2] This opinion seems actually to have been entertained by Adam Smith, the worst critic, David Hume not excepted, that Scotland, a soil to which this sort of weed seems natural, has produced.

[85]

whom he deems most worthy of his son's perusal, particularises only Lord Rochester, Sir John Denham, and Cowley. Writing about the same time, Shaftesbury, an author at present unjustly depreciated, describes the English Muses as only yet lisping in their cradles.

The arts by which Pope, soon afterwards, contrived to procure to himself a more general and a higher reputation than perhaps any English Poet ever attained during his lifetime, are known to the judicious. And as well known is it to them, that the undue exertion of those arts is the cause why Pope has for some time held a rank in literature, to which, if he had not been seduced by an over-love of immediate popularity, and had confided more in his native genius, he never could have descended. He bewitched the nation by his melody, and dazzled it by his polished style, and was himself blinded by his own success. Having wandered from humanity in his Eclogues with boyish inexperience, the praise which these compositions obtained tempted him into a belief that Nature was not to be trusted, at least in pastoral Poetry. To prove this by example, he put his friend Gay upon writing those Eclogues, which their author intended to be burlesque. The instigator of the work, and his admirers, could perceive in them nothing but what was ridiculous. Nevertheless, though these Poems contain some detestable passages, the effect, as Dr. Johnson well observes, "of reality and truth became conspicuous even when the intention was to show them grovelling and degraded." The Pastorals, ludicrous to such as prided themselves upon their refinement, in spite of those disgusting passages, "became popular, and were read with delight, as just representations of rural manners and occupations."

Something less than sixty years after the publication of the "Paradise Lost" appeared Thomson's "Winter"; which was speedily followed by his other Seasons. It is a work of inspiration; much of it is written from himself, and nobly from himself. How was it received? "It was no sooner read," says one of his contemporary biographers, "than universally admired: those only excepted who had not been used to feel, or to look for anything in poetry, beyond a *point* of satirical or epigrammatic wit, a smart *antithesis* richly trimmed with rhyme, or the softness of an *elegiac* complaint. To such his manly classical spirit could not readily commend itself; till, after a more attentive perusal, they had got the better of their prejudices, and either acquired or affected a truer taste. A few others stood aloof, merely because they had long before fixed the articles of their poetical creed, and resigned themselves to an absolute despair of ever seeing anything new and original. These were somewhat mortified to find their notions disturbed by the appearance of a poet, who seemed to owe nothing but to nature and his own genius. But, in a short time, the applause became unanimous; every one wondering how so many pictures, and pictures so familiar, should have moved them but faintly to what they felt in his descriptions. His digressions too, the overflowings of a tender benevolent heart, charmed the reader no less; leaving him in doubt, whether he should more admire the Poet or love the Man."

This case appears to bear strongly against us: — but we must distinguish between wonder and legitimate admiration. The subject of the work is the changes produced in the appearances of nature by the revolution of the year: and, by undertaking to write in verse, Thomson pledged himself to treat his subject as became a Poet. Now it is remarkable that, excepting the nocturnal "Reverie of Lady Winchilsea," and a passage or two in the "Windsor Forest" of Pope, the poetry of the period intervening between the publication of the "Paradise Lost" and the "Seasons" does not contain a single new image of external nature, and scarcely presents a familiar one from which it can be inferred that the eye of the Poet had been steadily fixed upon his object, much less that his feelings had urged him to work upon it in the spirit of genuine imagination. To what a low state knowledge of the most obvious and important phenomena had sunk, is evident from the style in which Dryden has executed a description of Night in one of his Tragedies, and Pope his translation of the celebrated moonlight scene in the Iliad. A blind man, in the habit of attending accurately to descriptions casually dropped from the lips of those around him, might easily depict these appearances with more truth. Dryden's lines are vague, bombastic, and senseless; [1] those of Pope, though he had Homer to guide him, are throughout false and contradictory. The verses of Dryden, once highly celebrated, are forgotten; those of Pope still retain their hold upon public estimation, — nay, there is not a passage of descriptive poetry, which at this day finds so many and such ardent admirers. Strange to think of an enthusiast, as may have been the case with thousands, reciting those verses under the cope of a moonlight sky, without having his raptures in the least disturbed by a suspicion of their absurdity! — If these two distinguished writers could habitually think that the visible universe was of so little conse-quence to a poet, that it was scarcely necessary for him to cast his eyes upon it, we may be assured that those passages of the elder poets which faithfully and poetic-ally describe the phenomena of nature, were not at that time holden in much estimation, and that there was little accurate attention paid to those appearances.

Wonder is the natural product of Ignorance; and as the soil was *in such good condition* at the time of the publication of the "Seasons," the crop was doubtless abundant. Neither individuals nor nations become

---

[1] CORTES *alone in a night-gown.*
   All things are hush'd as Nature's self lay dead;
   The mountains seem to nod their drowsy head.
   The little Birds in dreams their songs repeat,
   And sleeping Flowers beneath the Night-dew sweat:
   Even lust and Envy sleep; yet Love denies
   Rest to my soul, and slumber to my eyes.
                              DRYDEN's *Indian Emperor.*

corrupt all at once, nor are they enlightened in a moment. Thomson was an inspired poet, but he could not work miracles; in cases where the art of seeing had in some degree been learned, the teacher would further the proficiency of his pupils, but he could do little *more;* though so far does vanity assist men in acts of self-deception, that many would often fancy they recognised a likeness when they knew nothing of the original. Having shown that much of what his biographer deemed genuine admiration must in fact have been blind wonderment — how is the rest to be accounted for? — Thomson was fortunate in the very title of his poem, which seemed to bring it home to the prepared sympathies of every one: in the next place, notwithstanding his high powers, he writes a vicious style; and his false ornaments are exactly of that kind which would be most likely to strike the undiscerning. He likewise abounds with sentimental commonplaces that, from the manner in which they were brought forward, bore an imposing air of novelty. In any well-used copy of the "Seasons" the book generally opens of itself with the rhapsody on love, or with one of the stories (perhaps Damon and Musidora); these also are prominent in our collections of Extracts, and are the parts of his Work which, after all, were probably most efficient in first recommending the author to general notice. Pope, repaying praises which he had received, and wishing to extol him to the highest, only styles him "an elegant and philosophical Poet"; nor are we able to collect any unquestionable proofs that the true characteristics of Thomson's genius as an imaginative poet [1] were perceived, till the elder Warton, almost forty years after the publication of the "Seasons," pointed them out by a note in his *Essay on the Life and Writings of Pope*. In the "Castle of Indolence" (of which Gray speaks so coldly) these characteristics were almost as conspicuously displayed, and in verse more harmonious and diction more pure. Yet that fine poem was neglected on its appearance, and is at this day the delight only of a few!

When Thomson died, Collins breathed forth his regrets in an Elegiac Poem, in which he pronounces a poetical curse upon *him* who should regard with insensibility the place where the Poet's remains were deposited. The Poems of the mourner himself have now passed through innumerable editions, and are universally known; but if, when Collins died, the same kind of imprecation had been pronounced by a surviving admirer, small is the number whom it would not have comprehended. The notice which his poems attained during his lifetime was so small, and of course the sale so insignificant, that not long before his death he deemed it right to repay to the bookseller the sum which he had advanced for them, and threw the edition into the fire.

[1] Since these observations upon Thomson were written, I have perused the second edition of his "Seasons," and find that even that does not contain the most striking passages which Warton points out for admiration; these, with other improvements, throughout the whole work, must have been added at a later period.

Next in importance to the "Seasons" of Thomson, though at considerable distance from that work, in order of time, come the *Reliques of Ancient English Poetry*, collected, new-modelled, and in many instances (if such a contradiction in terms may be used) composed by the Editor, Dr. Percy. This work did not steal silently into the world, as is evident from the number of legendary tales that appeared not long after its publication; and had been modelled, as the authors persuaded themselves, after the old Ballad. The Compilation was however ill suited to the then existing taste of city society; and Dr. Johnson, 'mid the little senate to which he gave laws, was not sparing in his exertions to make it an object of contempt. The critic triumphed, the legendary imitators were deservedly disregarded, and, as undeservedly, their ill-imitated models sank, in this country, into temporary neglect; while Bürger, and other able writers of Germany, were translating or imitating these Reliques, and composing, with the aid of inspiration thence derived, poems which are the delight of the German nation. Dr. Percy was so abashed by the ridicule flung upon his labours from the ignorance and insensibility of the persons with whom he lived, that, though while he was writing under a mask he had not wanted resolution to follow his genius into the regions of true simplicity and genuine pathos (as is evinced by the exquisite ballad of Sir Cauline and by many other pieces), yet when he appeared in his own person and character as a poetical writer, he adopted, as in the tale of the Hermit of Warkworth, a diction scarcely in any one of its features distinguishable from the vague, the glossy, and unfeeling language of his day. I mention this remarkable fact [1] with regret, esteeming the genius of Dr. Percy in this kind of writing superior to that of any other man by whom in modern times it has been cultivated. That even Bürger (to whom Klopstock gave in my hearing a commendation which he denied to Goethe and Schiller, pronouncing him to be a genuine poet, and one of the few among the Germans whose works would last) had not the fine sensibility of Percy, might be shown from many passages, in which he has deserted his original only to go astray.

For example,

> " Now daye was gone, and night was come,
>   And all were fast asleepe,
>   All save the Lady Emeline,
>   Who sate in her bowre to weepe:
>   And soone she heard her true Love's voice
>   Low whispering at the walle,
>   Awake, awake, my dear Ladye,
>   'T is I thy true-love call."

---

[1] Shenstone, in his "Schoolmistress," gives a still more remarkable instance of this timidity. On its first appearance (see D'Israeli's 2d series of the *Curiosities of Literature*) the poem was accompanied with an absurd prose commentary, showing, as indeed some incongruous expressions in the text imply, that the whole was intended for burlesque. In subsequent editions the commentary was dropped, and the People have since continued to read in seriousness, doing for the Author what he had not courage openly to venture upon for himself.

[93]

Which is thus tricked out and dilated:

> "Als nun die Nacht Gebirg' und Thal
> Vermummt in Rabenschatten,
> Und Hochburgs Lampen überall
> Schon ausgeflimmert hatten,
> Und alles tief entschlafen war;
> Doch nur das Fräulein immerdar,
> Voll Fieberängst, noch wachte,
> Und seinen Ritter dachte:
> Da horch! Ein süssder Liebeston
> Kam leis' empor geflogen.
> 'Ho, Trudchen, ho! Da bin ich schon!
> Frisch auf! Dich angezogen!'"

But from humble ballads we must ascend to heroics.

All hail, Macpherson! hail to thee, Sire of Ossian! The Phantom was begotten by the snug embrace of an impudent Highlander upon a cloud of tradition — it travelled southward, where it was greeted with acclamation, and the thin Consistence took its course through Europe, upon the breath of popular applause. The Editor of the *Reliques* had indirectly preferred a claim to the praise of invention, by not concealing that his supplementary labours were considerable! how selfish his conduct, contrasted with that of the disinterested Gael, who, like Lear, gives his kingdom away, and is content to become a pensioner upon his own issue for a beggarly pittance! — Open this far-famed Book! — I have done so at random, and the beginning of the "Epic Poem Temora," in eight Books, presents itself. "The blue waves of Ullin roll in light. The green hills are covered with day. Trees shake their dusky heads in the breeze. Grey torrents pour their noisy streams. Two green hills with aged oaks surround a narrow plain. The blue course of a stream is there. On its banks stood Cairbar of Atha. His spear supports the king; the red eyes of his fear are sad. Cormac rises on his soul with all his ghastly wounds." Precious memorandums from the pocket-book of the blind Ossian!

If it be unbecoming, as I acknowledge that for the most part it is, to speak disrespectfully of Works that have enjoyed for a length of time a widely-spread reputation, without at the same time, producing irrefragable proofs of their unworthiness, let me be forgiven upon this occasion. — Having had the good fortune to be born and reared in a mountainous country, from my very childhood I have felt the falsehood that pervades the volumes imposed upon the world under the name of Ossian. From what I saw with my own eyes, I knew that the imagery was spurious. In nature everything is distinct, yet nothing defined into absolute independent singleness. In Macpherson's work, it is exactly the reverse; everything (that is not stolen) is in this manner defined, insulated, dislocated, deadened, — yet nothing distinct. It will always be so when words are substituted for things. To say that the characters never could exist, that the manners are impossible, and that a dream has more substance than the whole state of society, as there depicted, is doing nothing more than pronouncing a censure which Macpherson defied; when, with the steeps of Morven before his eyes, he could talk so familiarly of his Car-borne heroes; — of Morven, which, if one may judge from its appearance at the distance of a few miles, contains scarcely an acre of ground sufficiently accommodating for a sledge to be trailed along its surface. — Mr. Malcolm Laing has ably shown that the diction of this pretended translation is a motley assemblage from all quarters; but he is so fond of making out parallel passages as to call poor Macpherson to account for his "*ands*" and his "*buts!*" and he has weakened his argument by conducting it as if he thought that every striking resemblance was a *conscious* plagiarism. It is enough that the coincidences are too remarkable for its being probable or possible that they could arise in different minds without communication between them. Now as the Translators of the Bible, and Shakspeare, Milton, and Pope, could not be indebted to Macpherson, it follows that he must have owed his fine feathers to them; unless we are prepared gravely to assert, with Madame de Staël, that many of the characteristic beauties of our most celebrated English Poets are derived from the ancient Fingallian; in which case the modern translator would have been but giving back to Ossian his own. — It is consistent that Lucien Buonaparte, who could censure Milton for having surrounded Satan in the infernal regions with courtly and regal splendour, should pronounce the modern Ossian to be the glory of Scotland; — a country that has produced a Dunbar, a Buchanan, a Thomson, and a Burns! These opinions are of ill omen for the Epic ambition of him who has given them to the world.

Yet, much as those pretended treasures of antiquity have been admired, they have been wholly uninfluential upon the literature of the Country. No succeeding writer appears to have caught from them a ray of inspiration; no author, in the least distinguished, has ventured formally to imitate them — except the boy, Chatterton, on their first appearance. He had perceived, from the successful trials which he himself had made in literary forgery, how few critics were able to distinguish between a real ancient medal and a counterfeit of modern manufacture; and he set himself to the work of filling a magazine with *Saxon Poems*, — counterparts of those of Ossian, as like his as one of his misty stars is to another. This incapability to amalgamate with the literature of the Island is, in my estimation, a decisive proof that the book is essentially unnatural; nor should I require any other to demonstrate it to be a forgery, audacious as worthless. — Contrast, in this respect, the effect of Macpherson's publication with the *Reliques* of Percy, so unassuming, so modest in their pretensions! — I have already stated how much Germany is indebted to this latter work; and for our own country, its poetry has been absolutely redeemed by it. I do not think that there is an able writer in verse of the present day who would not be proud to acknowledge his obligations to the *Reliques;* I know that it is

so with my friends; and, for myself, I am happy in this
occasion to make a public avowal of my own.

Dr. Johnson, more fortunate in his contempt of the
labours of Macpherson than those of his modest friend,
was solicited not long after to furnish Prefaces, biographical and critical, for the works of some of the most
eminent English Poets. The booksellers took upon
themselves to make the collection; they referred probably to the most popular miscellanies, and, unquestionably, to their books of accounts; and decided upon the
claim of authors to be admitted into a body of the most
eminent from the familiarity of their names with the
readers of that day, and by the profits which, from the
sale of his works, each had brought and was bringing to
the Trade. The Editor was allowed a limited exercise
of discretion, and the Authors whom he recommended
are scarcely to be mentioned without a smile. We open
the volume of Prefatory Lives, and to our astonishment
the *first* name we find is that of Cowley! — What is
become of the morning-star of English Poetry? Where
is the bright Elizabethan constellation? Or, if names
be more acceptable than images, where is the ever-to-
be-honoured Chaucer? where is Spenser? where Sidney?
and, lastly, where he, whose rights as a poet, contradistinguished from those which he is universally allowed to possess as a dramatist, we have vindicated,
— where Shakspeare? — These, and a multitude of
others not unworthy to be placed near them, their contemporaries and successors, we have *not*. But in their

stead, we have (could better be expected when precedence was to be settled by an abstract of reputation
at any given period made, as in this case before us?)
Roscommon, and Stepney, and Phillips, and Walsh,
and Smith, and Duke, and King, and Spratt—Halifax,
Granville, Sheffield, Congreve, Broome, and other re-
puted Magnates — metrical writers utterly worthless
and useless, except for occasions like the present, when
their productions are referred to as evidence what a
small quantity of brain is necessary to procure a considerable stock of admiration, provided the aspirant will
accommodate himself to the likings and fashions of
his day.

As I do not mean to bring down this retrospect to
our own times, it may with propriety be closed at the
era of this distinguished event. From the literature
of other ages and countries, proofs equally cogent
might have been adduced, that the opinions announced
in the former part of this Essay are founded upon
truth. It was not an agreeable office, nor a prudent
undertaking, to declare them; but their importance
seemed to render it a duty. It may still be asked, where
lies the particular relation of what has been said to these
volumes? — The question will be easily answered
by the discerning Reader who is old enough to remember the taste that prevailed when some of these poems
were first published, seventeen years ago; who has also
observed to what degree the poetry of this Island has
since that period been coloured by them; and who is

further aware of the unremitting hostility with which, upon some principle or other, they have each and all been opposed. A sketch of my own notion of the constitution of Fame has been given; and as far as concerns myself, I have cause to be satisfied. The love, the admiration, the indifference, the slight, the aversion, and even the contempt, with which these Poems have been received, knowing as I do, the source within my own mind from which they have proceeded, and the labour and pains which, when labour and pains appeared needful, have been bestowed upon them, must all, if I think consistently, be received as pledges and tokens, bearing the same general impression, though widely different in value; — they are all proofs that for the present time I have not laboured in vain; and afford assurances, more or less authentic, that the products of my industry will endure.

If there be one conclusion more forcibly pressed upon us than another by the review which has been given of the fortunes and fate of poetical Works, it is this, — that every author, as far as he is great and at the same time *original*, has had the task of *creating* the taste by which he is to be enjoyed: so has it been, so will it continue to be. This remark was long since made to me by the philosophical Friend for the separation of whose poems from my own I have previously expressed my regret. The predecessors of an original Genius of a high order will have smoothed the way for all that he has in common with them; — and much he

Mrs. Wordsworth

will have in common; but, for what is peculiarly his own, he will be called upon to clear and often to shape his own road: — he will be in the condition of Hannibal among the Alps.

And where lies the real difficulty of creating that taste by which a truly original poet is to be relished? Is it in breaking the bonds of custom, in overcoming the prejudices of false refinement, and displacing the aversions of inexperience? Or, if he labour for an object which here and elsewhere I have proposed to myself, does it consist in divesting the reader of the pride that induces him to dwell upon those points wherein men differ from each other, to the exclusion of those in which all men are alike, or the same; and in making him ashamed of the vanity that renders him insensible of the appropriate excellence which civil arrangements, less unjust than might appear, and Nature illimitable in her bounty, have conferred on men who may stand below him in the scale of society? Finally, does it lie in establishing that dominion over the spirits of readers by which they are to be humbled and humanised, in order that they may be purified and exalted?

If these ends are to be attained by the mere communication of *knowledge*, it does *not* lie here. — TASTE, I would remind the reader, like IMAGINATION, is a word which has been forced to extend its services far beyond the point to which philosophy would have confined them. It is a metaphor, taken from a *passive* sense of the human body, and transferred to things which are

[101]

in their essence *not* passive, — to intellectual *acts* and *operations*. The word Imagination has been over-strained, from impulses honourable to mankind, to meet the demands of the faculty which is perhaps the noblest of our nature. In the instance of Taste, the process has been reversed; and from the prevalence of dispositions at once injurious and discreditable, being no other than that selfishness which is the child of apathy, — which, as Nations decline in productive and creative power, makes them value themselves upon a presumed refinement of judging. Poverty of language is the primary cause of the use which we make of the word Imagination; but the word Taste has been stretched to the sense which it bears in modern Europe by habits of self-conceit, inducing that inversion in the order of things whereby a passive faculty is made paramount among the faculties conversant with the fine arts. Proportion and congruity, the requisite knowledge being supposed, are subjects upon which taste may be trusted; it is competent to this office; — for in its intercourse with these the mind is *passive*, and is affected painfully or pleasurably as by an instinct. But the profound and the exquisite in feeling, the lofty and universal in thought and imagination; or, in ordinary language, the pathetic and the sublime; — are neither of them, accurately speaking, objects of a faculty which could ever without a sinking in the spirit of Nations have been designated by the metaphor — *Taste*. And why? Because without the exertion of a co-operating *power* in the mind of the

Reader, there can be no adequate sympathy with either of these emotions: without this auxiliary impulse, elevated or profound passion cannot exist.

Passion, it must be observed, is derived from a word which signifies *suffering;* but the connection which suffering has with effort, with exertion, and *action*, is immediate and inseparable. How strikingly is this property of human nature exhibited by the fact that, in popular language, to be in a passion is to be angry! — But,

> "Anger in hasty *words* or *blows*
> Itself discharges on its foes."

To be moved, then, by a passion, is to be excited, often to external, and always to internal, effort; whether for the continuance and strengthening of the passion, or for its suppression, accordingly as the course which it takes may be painful or pleasurable. If the latter, the soul must contribute to its support, or it never becomes vivid, — and soon languishes, and dies. And this brings us to the point. If every great poet with whose writings men are familiar, in the highest exercise of his genius, before he can be thoroughly enjoyed, has to call forth and to communicate *power*, this service, in a still greater degree, falls upon an original writer at his first appearance in the world. — Of genius the only proof is the act of doing well what is worthy to be done, and what was never done before: Of genius, in the fine arts, the only infallible sign is the widening the sphere of human sensibility for the delight, honour, and benefit of human nature. Genius is the introduction of a new element into the intellectual universe: or, if that be not allowed, it is the application of powers to objects on which they had not before been exercised, or the employment of them in such a manner as to produce effects hitherto unknown. What is all this but an advance, or a conquest, made by the soul of the poet? Is it to be supposed that the reader can make progress of this kind, like an Indian prince or general — stretched on his palanquin, and borne by slaves? No; he is invigorated and inspirited by his leader, in order that he may exert himself; for he cannot proceed in quiescence, he cannot be carried like a dead weight. Therefore to create taste is to call forth and bestow power, of which knowledge is the effect; and *there* lies the true difficulty.

As the pathetic participates of an *animal* sensation, it might seem that, if the springs of this emotion were genuine, all men, possessed of competent knowledge of the facts and circumstances, would be instantaneously affected. And, doubtless, in the works of every true poet will be found passages of that species of excellence which is proved by effects immediate and universal. But there are emotions of the pathetic that are simple and direct, and others that are complex and revolutionary; some to which the heart yields with gentleness; others against which it struggles with pride; these varieties are.infinite as the combinations of circumstances and the constitutions of character. Remember, also, that the medium through which, in poetry, the heart is to be affected is language; a thing subject to endless fluctuations and arbitrary associations. The genius of the poet melts these down for his purpose; but they retain their shape and quality to him who is not capable of exerting, within his own mind, a corresponding energy. There is also a meditative, as well as a human, pathos; an enthusiastic as well as an ordinary sorrow; a sadness that has its seat in the depths of reason, to which the mind cannot sink gently of itself — but to which it must descend by treading the steps of thought. And for the sublime, — if we consider what are the cares that occupy the passing day, and how remote is the practice and the course of life from the sources of sublimity in the soul of Man, can it be wondered that there is little existing preparation for a poet charged with a new mission to extend its kingdom, and to augment and spread its enjoyments?

Away, then, with the senseless iteration of the word *popular* applied to new works in poetry, as if there were no test of excellence in this first of the fine arts but that all men should run after its productions, as if urged by an appetite, or constrained by a spell! — The qualities of writing best fitted for eager reception are either such as startle the world into attention by their audacity and extravagance; or they are chiefly of a superficial kind, lying upon the surfaces of manners; or arising out of a selection and arrangement of incidents, by which the mind is kept upon the stretch of curiosity, and the fancy amused without the trouble of thought. But in

[105]

everything which is to send the soul into herself, to be admonished of her weakness, or to be made conscious of her power; wherever life and nature are described as operated upon by the creative or abstracting virtue of the imagination; wherever the instinctive wisdom of antiquity and her heroic passions uniting, in the heart of the poet, with the meditative wisdom of later ages, have produced that accord of sublimated humanity, which is at once a history of the remote past and a prophetic enunciation of the remotest future; *there*, the poet must reconcile himself for a season to few and scattered hearers. — Grand thoughts (and Shakspeare must often have sighed over this truth), as they are most naturally and most fitly conceived in solitude, so can they not be brought forth in the midst of plaudits without some violation of their sanctity. Go to a silent exhibition of the productions of the sister Art, and be convinced that the qualities which dazzle at first sight, and kindle the admiration of the multitude, are essentially different from those by which permanent influence is secured. Let us not shrink from following up these principles as far as they will carry us, and conclude with observing that there never has been a period, and perhaps never will be, in which vicious poetry, of some kind or other, has not excited more zealous admiration, and been far more generally read, than good; but this advantage attends the good, that the *individual*, as well as the species, survives from age to age; whereas, of the depraved, though the species be immortal, the individual quickly *perishes;* the object of present admiration vanishes, being supplanted by some other as easily produced; which, though no better, brings with it at least the irritation of novelty, — with adaptation, more or less skilful, to the changing humours of the majority of those who are most at leisure to regard poetical works when they first solicit their attention.

Is it the result of the whole that, in the opinion of the Writer, the judgment of the People is not to be respected? The thought is most injurious; and, could the charge be brought against him, he would repel it with indignation. The people have already been justified, and their eulogium pronounced by implication, when it was said above that, of *good* poetry, the *individual*, as well as the species, *survives*. And how does it survive but through the People? What preserves it but their intellect and their wisdom?

> "—— Past and future, are the wings
> On whose support, harmoniously conjoined,
> Moves the great Spirit of human knowledge ——"
>
> *MS.*

The voice that issues from this spirit, is that Vox Populi which the Deity inspires. Foolish must be he who can mistake for this a local acclamation, or a transitory outcry — transitory though it be for years, local though from a Nation. Still more lamentable is his error who can believe that there is anything of divine infallibility in the clamour of that small though loud portion of the community, ever governed by factitious influence which, under the name of the PUBLIC, passes itself, upon the unthinking, for the PEOPLE. Towards the Public, the Writer hopes that he feels as much deference as it is entitled to: but to the People, philosophically characterised, and to the embodied spirit of their knowledge, so far as it exists and moves, at the present, faithfully supported by its two wings, the past and the future, his devout respect, his reverence, is due. He offers it willingly and readily; and, this done, takes leave of his Readers, by assuring them that, if he were not persuaded that the contents of these Volumes, and the work to which they are subsidiary, evince something of the "Vision and the Faculty divine"; and that, both in words and things, they will operate in their degree to extend the domain of sensibility for the delight, the honour, and the benefit of human nature, notwithstanding the many happy hours which he has employed in their composition, and the manifold comforts and enjoyments they have procured to him, he would not, if a wish would do it, save them from immediate destruction — from becoming at this moment, to the world, as a thing that had never been.

POSTSCRIPT

1835

In the present Volume, as in those that have preceded it, the reader will have found occasionally opinions expressed upon the course of public affairs, and feelings given vent to as national interests excited them. Since nothing, I trust, has been uttered but in the spirit of reflective patriotism, those notices are left to produce their own effect; but, among the many objects of general concern, and the changes going forward, which I have glanced at in verse, are some especially affecting the lower orders of society: in reference to these, I wish here to add a few words in plain prose.

Were I conscious of being able to do justice to those important topics, I might avail myself of the periodical press for offering anonymously my thoughts, such as they are, to the world; but I feel that in procuring attention, they may derive some advantage, however small, from my name, in addition to that of being presented in a less fugitive shape. It is also not impossible that the state of mind which some of the foregoing poems may have produced in the reader, will dispose him to receive more readily the impression which I desire to make, and to admit the conclusions I would establish.

POSTSCRIPT

I. The first thing that presses upon my attention is the Poor-Law Amendment Act. I am aware of the magnitude and complexity of the subject, and the unwearied attention which it has received from men of far wider experience than my own; yet I cannot forbear touching upon one point of it, and to this I will confine myself, though not insensibly to the objection which may reasonably be brought against treating a portion of this, or any other, great scheme of civil polity separately from the whole. The point to which I wish to draw the reader's attention is, that *all* persons who cannot find employment, or procure wages sufficient to support the body in health and strength, are entitled to a maintenance by law.

This dictate of humanity is acknowledged in the Report of the Commissioners: but is there not room for apprehension that some of the regulations of the new act have a tendency to render the principle nugatory by difficulties thrown in the way of applying it? If this be so, persons will not be wanting to show it, by examining the provisions of the act in detail, — an attempt which would be quite out of place here; but it will not, therefore, be deemed unbecoming in one who fears that the prudence of the head may, in framing some of those provisions, have supplanted the wisdom of the heart, to enforce a principle which cannot be violated without infringing upon one of the most precious rights of the English people, and opposing one of the most sacred claims of civilised humanity.

POSTSCRIPT

There can be no greater error, in this department of legislation, than the belief that this principle does by necessity operate for the degradation of those who claim, or are so circumstanced as to make it likely they may claim, through laws founded upon it, relief or assistance. The direct contrary is the truth: it may be unanswerably maintained that its tendency is to raise, not to depress; by stamping a value upon life, which can belong to it only where the laws have placed men who are willing to work, and yet cannot find employment, above the necessity of looking for protection against hunger and other natural evils, either to individual and casual charity, to despair and death, or to the breach of law by theft or violence.

And here, as in the Report of the Commissioners, the fundamental principle has been recognised, I am not at issue with them any farther than I am compelled to believe that their "remedial measures" obstruct the application of it more than the interests of society require.

And, calling to mind the doctrines of political economy which are now prevalent, I cannot forbear to enforce the justice of the principle, and to insist upon its salutary operation.

And first for its justice: If self-preservation be the first law of our nature, would not every one in a state of nature be morally justified in taking to himself that which is indispensable to such preservation, where, by so doing, he would not rob another of that which might be equally indispensable to *his* preservation? And if the value of life be regarded in a right point of view, may it not be questioned whether this right of preserving life, at any expense short of endangering the life of another, does not survive man's entering into the social state; whether this right can be surrendered or forfeited, except when it opposes the divine law, upon any supposition of a social compact, or of any convention for the protection of mere rights of property?

But if it be not safe to touch the abstract question of man's right in a social state to help himself even in the last extremity, may we not still contend for the duty of a christian government, standing *in loco parentis* towards all its subjects, to make such effectual provision, that no one shall be in danger of perishing either through the neglect or harshness of its legislation? Or, waiving this, is it not indisputable that the claim of the state to the allegiance involves the protection of the subject? And, as all rights in one party impose a correlative duty upon another, it follows that the right of the state to require the services of its members, even to the jeoparding of their lives in the common defence, establishes a right in the people (not to be gainsaid by utilitarians and economists) to public support when from any cause they may be unable to support themselves.

Let us now consider the salutary and benign operation of this principle. Here we must have recourse to elementary feelings of human nature, and to truths which from their very obviousness are apt to be slighted, till they are forced upon our notice by our own sufferings or those of others. In the "Paradise Lost," Milton represents Adam, after the Fall, as exclaiming in the anguish of his soul —

> "Did I request Thee, Maker, from my clay
> To mould me man; did I solicit Thee
> From darkness to promote me?
> .   .   .   .   .   .   My will
> Concurred not to my being."

Under how many various pressures of misery have men been driven thus, in a strain touching upon impiety, to expostulate with the Creator! and under few so afflictive as when the source and origin of earthly existence have been brought back to the mind by its impending close in the pangs of destitution. But as long as, in our legislation, due weight shall be given to this principle, no man will be forced to bewail the gift of life in hopeless want of the necessaries of life.

Englishmen have, therefore, by the progress of civilisation among them, been placed in circumstances more favourable to piety and resignation to the divine will than the inhabitants of other countries, where a like provision has not been established. And as Providence, in his care of our countrymen, acts through a human medium, the objects of that care must, in like manner, be more inclined towards a grateful love of their fellow-men. Thus, also, do stronger ties attach the people to their country, whether while they tread its soil, or, at a distance, think of their native land as an indulgent parent, to whose arms even they who have been imprudent and undeserving may, like the prodigal son, betake themselves, without fear of being rejected.

Such is the view of the case that would first present itself to a reflective mind; and it is in vain to show, by appeals to experience, in contrast with this view, that provisions founded upon the principle have promoted profaneness of life and dispositions the reverse of philanthropic, by spreading idleness, selfishness, and rapacity: for these evils have arisen, not as an inevitable consequence of the principle, but for want of judgment in framing laws based upon it; and, above all, from faults, in the mode of administering the law. The mischief that has grown to such a height from granting relief in cases where proper vigilance would have shown that it was not required, or in bestowing it in undue measure, will be urged by no truly enlightened statesman as a sufficient reason for banishing the principle itself from legislation.

Let us recur to the miserable states of consciousness that it precludes.

There is a story told, by a traveller in Spain, of a female who, by a sudden shock of domestic calamity, was driven out of her senses, and ever after looked up incessantly to the sky, feeling that her fellow-creatures could do nothing for her relief. Can there be Englishmen who, with a good end in view, would, upon system, expose their brother Englishmen to a like necessity of looking upwards only; or downwards to the earth, after it shall contain no spot where the destitute can demand, by civil right, what by right of nature they are entitled to?

Suppose the objects of our sympathy not sunk into this blank despair, but wandering about as strangers in streets and ways, with the hope of succour from casual charity; what have we gained by such a change of scene? Woful is the condition of the famished Northern Indian, dependent, among winter snows, upon the chance-passage of a herd of deer, from which one, if brought down by his rifle-gun, may be made the means of keeping him and his companions alive. As miserable is that of some savage islander, who, when the land has ceased to afford him sustenance, watches for food which the waves may cast up, or in vain endeavours to extract it from the inexplorable deep. But neither of these is in state of wretchedness comparable to that which is so often endured in civilised society: multitudes, in all ages, have known it, of whom may be said: —

> "Homeless, near a thousand homes they stood,
> And near a thousand tables pined, and wanted food."

Justly might I be accused of wasting time in an uncalled for attempt to excite the feelings of the reader, if systems of political economy, widely spread, did not impugn the principle, and if the safeguards against such extremities were left unimpaired. It is broadly asserted by many, that every man who endeavours to find work *may* find it: were this assertion capable of being verified, there still would remain a question, what kind of work,

[115]

and how far may the labourer be fit for it? For if sedentary work is to be exchanged for standing, and some light and nice exercise of the fingers, to which an artisan has been accustomed all his life, for severe labour of the arms, the best efforts would turn to little account, and occasion would be given for the unthinking and the unfeeling unwarrantably to reproach those who are put upon such employment as idle, froward, and unworthy of relief, either by law or in any other way! Were this statement correct, there would indeed be an end of the argument, the principle here maintained would be superseded, But, alas! it is far otherwise. That principle, applicable to the benefit of all countries, is indispensable for England, upon whose coast families are perpetually deprived of their support by shipwreck, and where large masses of men are so liable to be thrown out of their ordinary means of gaining bread, by changes in commercial intercourse, subject mainly or solely to the will of foreign powers; by new discoveries in arts and manufactures; and by reckless laws, in conformity with theories of political economy, which, whether right or wrong, in the abstract, have proved a scourge to tens of thousands by the abruptness with which they have been carried into practice.

But it is urged, — refuse altogether compulsory relief to the able-bodied, and the number of those who stand in need of relief will steadily diminish through a conviction of an absolute necessity for greater forethought and more prudent care of a man's earnings.

Undoubtedly it would, but so also would it, and in a much greater degree, if the legislative provisions were retained, and parochial relief administered under the care of the upper classes, as it ought to be. For it has been invariably found, that wherever the funds have been raised and applied under the superintendence of gentlemen and substantial proprietors, acting in vestries and as overseers, pauperism has diminished accordingly. Proper care in that quarter would effectually check what is felt in some districts to be one of the worst evils in the poor law system, viz. the readiness of small and needy proprietors to join in imposing rates that seemingly subject them to great hardships, while, in fact, this is done with a mutual understanding that the relief each is ready to bestow upon his still poorer neighbours will be granted to himself, or his relatives, should it hereafter be applied for.

But let us look to inner sentiments of a nobler quality, in order to know what we have to build upon. Affecting proofs occur in every one's experience, who is acquainted with the unfortunate and the indigent, of their unwillingness to derive their subsistence from aught but their own funds or labour or to be indebted to parochial assistance for the attainment of any object, however dear to them. A case was reported, the other day, from a coroner's inquest, of a pair who, through the space of four years, had carried about their dead infant from house to house, and from lodging to lodging, as their necessities drove them, rather than ask the parish to bear the expense of its interment: — the poor creatures lived in the hope of one day being able to bury their child at their own cost. It must have been heart-rendering to see and hear the mother, who had been called upon to account for the state in which the body was found, make this deposition. By some, judging coldly, if not harshly, this conduct might be imputed to an unwarrantable pride, as she and her husband had, it is true, been once in prosperity. But examples, where the spirit of independence works with equal strength, though not with like miserable accompaniments, are frequently to be found even yet among the humblest peasantry and mechanics. There is not, then, sufficient cause for doubting that a like sense of honour may be revived among the people, and their ancient habits of independence restored, without resorting to those severities which the new Poor Law Act has introduced.

But even if the surfaces of things only are to be examined, we have a right to expect that lawgivers should take into account the various tempers and dispositions of mankind: while some are led, by the existence of a legislative provision, into idleness and extravagance, the economical virtues might be cherished in others by the knowledge that, if all their efforts fail, they have in the Poor Laws a "refuge from the storm and a shadow from the heat." Despondency and distraction are no friends to prudence: the springs of industry will relax, if cheerfulness be destroyed by anxiety; without hope men become reckless, and have a sullen pride in adding to the heap of their own wretchedness. He who feels that he is abandoned by his fellowmen will be almost irresistibly driven to care little for himself; will lose his self-respect accordingly, and with that loss what remains to him of virtue?

With all due deference to the particular experience and general intelligence of the individuals who framed the Act, and of those who in and out of parliament have approved of and supported it, it may be said that it proceeds too much upon the presumption that it is a labouring man's own fault if he be not, as the phrase is, beforehand with the world. But the most prudent are liable to be thrown back by sickness, cutting them off from labour, and causing to them expense; and who but has observed how distress creeps upon multitudes without misconduct of their own; and merely from a gradual fall in the price of labour, without a correspondent one in the price of provisions; so that men who may have ventured upon the marriage state with a fair prospect of maintaining their families in comfort and happiness, see them reduced to a pittance which no effort of theirs can increase? Let it be remembered, also, that there are thousands with whom vicious habits of expense are not the cause why they do not store up their gains; but they are generous and kind-hearted, and ready to help their kindred and friends; moreover, they have a faith in Providence that those who have been prompt to assist others, will not be left destitute, should they themselves come to need. By acting from these blended feelings, numbers have rendered themselves incapable of standing up against a sudden reverse. Nevertheless, these men, in common with all who have the misfortune to be in want, if many theorists had their wish, would be thrown upon one or other of those three sharp points of condition before adverted to, from which the intervention of law has hitherto saved them.

All that has been said tends to show how the principle contended for makes the gift of life more valuable, and has, it may be hoped, led to the conclusion that its legitimate operation is to make men worthier of that gift: in other words, not to degrade but to exalt human nature. But the subject must not be dismissed without adverting to the indirect influence of the same principle upon the moral sentiments of a people among whom it is embodied in law. In our criminal jurisprudence there is a maxim, deservedly eulogised, that it is better that ten guilty persons shall escape, than that one innocent man should suffer; so, also, might it be maintained, with regard to the Poor Laws, that it is better for the interests of humanity among the people at large, that ten undeserving should partake of the funds provided, than that one morally good man, through want of relief, should either have his principles corrupted or his energies destroyed; than that such a one should either be driven to do wrong or be cast to the earth in utter hopelessness. In France the English maxim of criminal jurisprudence is reversed; there, it is deemed better that ten

innocent men should suffer than one guilty escape:
in France there is no universal provision for the poor;
and we may judge of the small value set upon human
life in the metropolis of that country, by merely not-
icing the disrespect with which, after death, the body
is treated, not by the thoughtless vulgar, but in schools
of anatomy, presided over by men allowed to be, in
their own art and in physical science, among the most
enlightened in the world. In the East, where countries
are overrun with population as with a weed, infinitely
more respect is shown to the remains of the deceased;
and what a bitter mockery is it, that this insensibility
should be found where civil polity is so busy in minor
regulations, and ostentatiously careful to gratify the
luxurious propensities, whether social or intellectual,
of the multitude! Irreligion is, no doubt, much con-
cerned with this offensive disrespect shown to the bodies
of the dead in France; but it is mainly attributable to
the state in which so many of the living are left by the
absence of compulsory provision for the indigent so
humanely established by the law of England.

Sights of abject misery, perpetually recurring, harden
the heart of the community. In the perusal of history
and of works of fiction we are not, indeed, unwilling to
have our commisseration excited by such objects of distress as they present to us; but, in the concerns of real
life, men know that such emotions are not given to
be indulged for their own sakes: there, the conscience
declares to them that sympathy must be followed by

action; and if there exist a previous conviction that the power to relieve is utterly inadequate to the demand, the eye shrinks from communication with wretchedness, and pity and compassion languish, like any other qualities that are deprived of their natural aliment. Let these considerations be duly weighed by those who trust to the hope that an increase of private charity, with all its advantages of superior discrimination, would more than compensate for the abandonment of those principles, the wisdom of which has been here insisted upon. How discouraging, also, would be the sense of injustice, which could not fail to arise in the minds of the well-disposed, if the burden of supporting the poor, a burden of which the selfish have hitherto by compulsion borne a share, should now, or hereafter, be thrown exclusively upon the benevolent.

By having put an end to the Slave Trade and Slavery, the British people are exalted in the scale of humanity; and they cannot but feel so, if they look into themselves, and duly consider their relation to God and their fellow-creatures. That was a noble advance; but a retrograde movement will assuredly be made, if ever the principle which has been here defended should be either avowedly abandoned or but ostensibly retained.

But, after all, there may be a little reason to apprehend permanent injury from any experiment that may be tried. On the one side will be human nature rising up in her own defence and on the other prudential selfishness acting to the same purpose, from a conviction that, without a compulsory provision for the exigencies of the labouring multitude, that degree of ability to regulate the price of labour, which is indispensable for the reasonable interest of arts and manufactures, cannot, in Great Britain, be upheld.

II. In a poem of the foregoing collection allusion is made to the state of the workmen congregated in manufactories. In order to relieve many of the evils to which that class of society are subject, and to establish a better harmony between them and their employers, it would be well to repeal such laws as prevent the formation of joint-stock companies. There are, no doubt, many and great obstacles to the formation and salutary working of these societies, inherent in the mind of those whom they would obviously benefit. But the combinations of masters to keep down, unjustly, the price of labour would be fairly checked by them, as far as they were practicable; they would encourage economy, inasmuch as they would enable a man to draw profit from his savings, by investing them in buildings or machinery for processes of manufacture with which he was habitually connected. His little capital would then be working for him while he was at rest or asleep; he would more clearly perceive the necessity of capital for carrying on great works; he would better learn to respect the larger portions of it in the hands of others; he would be less tempted to join in unjust combinations; and, for the sake of his own property, if not for higher reasons, he would be slow to promote local disturbance or endanger public tranquillity; he would, at least, be loth to act in that way *knowingly:* for it is not to be denied that such societies might be nurseries of opinions unfavourable to a mixed constitution of government, like that of Great Britain. The democratic and republican spirit which they might be apt to foster would not, however, be dangerous in itself, but only as it might act without being sufficiently counterbalanced, either by landed proprietorship, or by a Church extending itself so as to embrace an ever-growing and ever-shifting population of mechanics and artisans. But if the tendencies of such societies would be to make the men prosper who might belong to them, rulers and legislators should rejoice in the result, and do their duty to the state by upholding and extending the influence of that Church, to which it owes, in so great a measure, its safety, its prosperity, and its glory.

This, in the temper of the present times, may be difficult, but it is become indispensable, since large towns in great numbers have sprung up, and others have increased tenfold, with little or no dependence upon the gentry and the landed proprietors; and apart from those mitigated feudal institutions, which, till of late, have acted so powerfully upon the composition of the House of Commons. Now it may be affirmed that, in quarters where there is not an attachment to the Church, or the landed aristocracy, and a pride in supporting them, *there* the people will dislike both, and be ready, upon such incitements as are perpetually recurring, to join in attempts to overthrow them. There is no neutral ground here: from want of due attention to the state of society in large towns and manufacturing districts, and ignorance or disregard of these obvious truths, innumerable well-meaning persons became zealous supporters of a Reform Bill, the qualities and powers of which, whether destructive or constructive, they would otherwise have been afraid of; and even the framers of that bill, swayed as they might be by party resentments and personal ambition, could not have gone so far, had not they too been lamentably ignorant or neglectful of the same truths both of fact and philosophy.

But let that pass; and let no opponent of the bill be tempted to compliment his own foresight, by exaggerating the mischiefs and dangers that have sprung from it: let not time be wasted in profitless regrets; and let those party distinctions vanish to their very names that have separated men who, whatever course they may have pursued, have ever had a bond of union in the wish to save the limited monarchy and those other institutions that have, under Providence, rendered for so long a period of time this country the happiest and worthiest of which there is any record since the foundation of civil society.

III. A philosophic mind is best pleased when looking at religion in its spiritual bearing; as a guide of conduct, a solace under affliction, and a support amid the instabilities of mortal life: but the Church having been forcibly brought by political considerations to my notice, while treating of the labouring classes, I cannot forbear saying a few words upon that momentous topic.

There is a loud clamour for extensive change in that department. The clamour would be entitled to more respect if they who are the most eager to swell it with their voices were not generally the most ignorant of the real state of the Church and the service it renders to the community. *Reform* is the word employed. Let us pause and consider what sense it is apt to carry, and how things are confounded by a lax use of it. The great religious Reformation, in the sixteenth century, did not profess to be a new construction, but a restoration of something fallen into decay, or put out of sight. That familiar and justifiable use of the word seems to have paved the way for fallacies with respect to the term reform, which it is difficult to escape from. Were we to speak of improvement and the correction of abuses we should run less risk of being deceived ourselves or of misleading others. We should be less likely to fall blindly into the belief that the change demanded is a renewal of something that has existed before, and that, therefore, we have experience on our side; nor should we be equally tempted to beg the question that the change for which we are eager must be advantageous. From generation to generation, men are the dupes of words;

and it is painful to observe that so many of our species are most tenacious of those opinions which they have formed with the least consideration. They who are the readiest to meddle with public affairs, whether in church or state, fly to generalities, that they may be eased from the trouble of thinking about particulars; and thus is deputed to mechanical instrumentality the work which vital knowledge only can do well.

"Abolish pluralities, have a resident incumbent in every parish," is a favourite cry; but, without adverting to other obstacles in the way of this specious scheme, it may be asked what benefit would accrue from its *indiscriminate* adoption to counterbalance the harm it would introduce, by nearly extinguishing the order of curates, unless the revenues of the church should grow with the population, and be greatly increased in many thinly-peopled districts, especially among the parishes of the North.

The order of curates is so beneficial, that some particular notice of it seems to be required in this place. For a church poor as, relatively to the numbers of people, that of England is, and probably will continue to be, it is no small advantage to have youthful servants who will work upon the wages of hope and expectation. Still more advantageous is it to have, by means of this order, young men scattered over the country, who being more detached from the temporal concerns of the benefice, have more leisure for improvement and study, and are less subject to be brought into secular collision with those who are under their spiritual guardianship. The curate, if he reside at a distance from the incumbent, undertakes the requisite responsibilities of a temporal kind, in that modified way which prevents him, as a new-comer, from being charged with selfishness: while it prepares him for entering upon a benefice of his own with something of a suitable experience. If he should act under and in co-operation with a resident incumbent, the gain is mutual. His studies will probably be assisted; and his training, managed by a superior, will not be liable to relapse in matters of prudence, seemliness, or in any of the highest cares of his functions; and by way of return for these benefits to the pupil, it will often happen that the zeal of a middle-aged or declining incumbent will be revived, by being in near communion with the ardour of youth, when his own efforts may have languished through a melancholy consciousness that they have not produced as much good among his flock as, when he first entered upon the charge, he fondly hoped.

Let one remark, and that not the least important, be added. A curate, entering for the first time upon his office, comes from college after a course of expense, and with such inexperience in the use of money that in his new situation he is apt to fall unawares into pecuniary difficulties. If this happens to him, much more likely is it to happen to the youthful incumbent, whose relations, to his parishioners and to society, are more complicated; and, his income being larger and independent of another, a costlier style of living is required of him by public opinion. If embarrassment should ensue, and with that unavoidably some loss of respectability, his future usefulness will be proportionably impaired: not so with the curate, for he can easily remove and start afresh with a stock of experience and an unblemished reputation; whereas the early indiscretions of an incumbent being rarely forgotten, may be impediments to the efficacy of his ministry for the remainder of his life. The same observations would apply with equal force to doctrine. A young minister is liable to errors, from his notions being either too lax or overstrained. In both cases it would prove injurious that the error should be remembered, after study and reflection, with advancing years, shall have brought him to a clearer discernment of the truth, and better judgment in the application of it.

It must be acknowledged that, among the regulations of ecclesiastical polity, none at first view are more attractive than that which prescribes for every parish a resident incumbent. How agreeable to picture to one's self, as has been done by poets and romance-writers, from Chaucer down to Goldsmith, a man devoted to his ministerial office, with not a wish or a thought ranging beyond the circuit of its cares! Nor is it in poetry and fiction only that such characters are found; they are scattered, it is hoped not sparingly, over real life, especially in sequestered and rural districts, where there is but small influx of new inhabitants, and little change ᴛ

of occupation. The spirit of the Gospel, unaided by acquisitions of profane learning and experience in the world, — that spirit and the obligations of the sacred office may, in such situations, suffice to effect most of what is needful. But for the complex state of society that prevails in England much more is required, both in large towns and in many extensive districts of the country. A minister there should not only be irreproachable in manners and morals, but accomplished in learning, as far as is possible without sacrifice of the least of his pastoral duties. As necessary, perhaps more so, is it that he should be a citizen as well as a scholar; thoroughly acquainted with the structure of society and the constitution of civil government, and able to reason upon both with the most expert; all ultimately in order to support the truths of Christianity and to diffuse its blessings.

A young man coming fresh from the place of his education cannot have brought with him these accomplishments; and if the scheme of equalising church incomes, which many advisers are much bent upon, be realised, so that there should be little or no secular inducement for a clergyman to desire a removal from the spot where he may chance to have been first set down; surely not only opportunities for obtaining the requisite qualifications would be diminished, but the motives for desiring to obtain them would be proportionately weakened. And yet these qualifications are indispensable for the diffusion of that knowledge by which alone the political philosophy of the New Testament can be rightly expounded, and its precepts adequately enforced. In these times, when the press is daily exercising so great a power over the minds of the people, for wrong or for right as may happen, *that* preacher ranks among the first of benefactors who, without stooping to the direct treatment of current politics and passing events, can furnish infallible guidance through the delusions that surround them; and who, appealing to the sanctions of Scripture, may place the grounds of its injunctions in so clear a light that disaffection shall cease to be cultivated as a laudable propensity, and loyalty cleansed from the dishonour of a blind and prostrate obedience.

It is not, however, in regard to civic duties alone, that this knowledge in a minister of the Gospel is important; it is still more so for softening and subduing private and personal discontents. In all places, and at all times, men have gratuitously troubled themselves, because their survey of the dispensations of Providence has been partial and narrow; but now that readers are so greatly multiplied, men judge as they are *taught*, and repinings are engendered everywhere, by imputations being cast upon the government; and are prolonged or aggravated by being ascribed to misconduct or injustice in rulers, when the individual himself only is in fault. If a Christian pastor be competent to deal with these humours, as they may be dealt with, and by no members of society so successfully, both from more frequent and more favourable opportunities of inter-course, and by aid of the authority with which he speaks; he will be a teacher of moderation, a dispenser of the wisdom that blunts approaching distress by submission to God's will, and lightens, by patience, grievances which cannot be removed.

We live in times when nothing, of public good at least, is generally acceptable, but what we believe can be traced to preconceived intention and specific acts and formal contrivances of human understanding. A Christian instructor thoroughly accomplished would be a standing restraint upon such presumptuousness of judgment, by impressing the truth that

> "In the unreasoning progress of the world
> A wiser spirit is at work for us,
> A better eye than ours."

MS.

Revelation points to the purity and peace of a future world; but our sphere of duty is upon earth; and the revelations of impure and conflicting things to each other must be understood, or we shall be perpetually going wrong, in all but goodness of intention; and good-ness of intention will itself relax through frequent dis-appointment. How desirable, then, is it, that a minis-ter of the Gospel should be versed in the knowledge of existing facts, and be accustomed to a wide range of social experience! Nor is it less desirable for the purpose of counterbalancing and tempering in his own mind that ambition with which spiritual power is as apt to be tainted as any other species of power which men covet or possess.

It must be obvious that the scope of the argument is to discourage an attempt which would introduce into the Church of England an equality of income and station upon the model of that of Scotland. The sounder part of the Scottish nation know what good their ancestors derived from their church, and feel how deeply the living generation is indebted to it. They respect and love it, as accommodated in so great a measure to a comparatively poor country, through the far greater portion of which prevails a uniformity of employment; but the acknowledged deficiency of theological learning among the clergy of that church is easily accounted for by this very equality. What else may be wanting there it would be unpleasant to inquire, and might prove invidious to determine: one thing, however, is clear; that in all countries the temporalities of the Church Establishment should bear an analogy to the state of society, otherwise it cannot diffuse its influence through the whole community. In a country so rich and luxurious as England, the character of its clergy must unavoidably sink, and their influence be everywhere impaired, if individuals from the upper ranks, and men of leading talents, are to have no inducements to enter into that body but such as are purely spiritual. And this "tinge of secularity" is no reproach to the clergy, nor does it imply a deficiency of spiritual endowments. Parents and guardians, looking forward to sources of

[133]

honourable maintenance for their children and wards, often direct their thoughts early towards the church, being determined partly by outward circumstances, and partly by indications of seriousness or intellectual fitness. It is natural that a boy or youth, with such a prospect before him, should turn his attention to those studies, and be led into those habits of reflection, which will in some degree tend to prepare him for the duties he is hereafter to undertake. As he draws nearer to the time when he will be called to these duties, he is both led and compelled to examine the Scriptures. He becomes more and more sensible of their truth. Devotion grows in him; and what might begin in temporal considerations, will end (as in a majority of instances we trust it does) in a spiritual-mindedness not unworthy of that Gospel, the lessons of which he is to teach, and the faith of which he is to inculcate. Not inappositely may be here repeated an observation which, from its obviousness and importance, must have been frequently made, viz., that the impoverishing of the clergy, and bringing their incomes much nearer to a level, would not cause them to become less worldly-minded: the emoluments, howsoever reduced, would be as eagerly sought for, but by men from lower classes in society; men who, by their manners, habits, abilities, and the scanty measure of their attainments, would unavoidably be less fitted for their station, and less competent to discharge its duties.

Visionary notions have in all ages been afloat upon

the subject of best providing for the clergy; notions which have been sincerely entertained by good men, with a view to the improvement of that order, and eagerly caught at and dwelt upon by the designing, for its degradation and disparagement. Some are beguiled by what they call the *voluntary system*, not seeing (what stares one in the face at the very threshold) that they who stand in most need of religious instruction are unconscious of the want, and therefore cannot reasonably be expected to make any sacrifices in order to supply it. Will the licentious, the sensual, and the depraved, take from the means of their gratifications and pursuits, to support a discipline that cannot advance without uprooting the trees that bear the fruit which they devour so greedily? Will *they* pay the price of that seed whose harvest is to be reaped in an invisible world? A voluntary system for the religious exigencies of a people numerous and circumstanced as we are! Not more absurd would it be to expect that a knot of boys should draw upon the pittance of their pocket-money to build schools, or out of the abundance of their discretion be able to select fit masters to teach and keep them in order! Some, who clearly perceive the incompetence and folly of such a scheme for the agricultural part of the people, nevertheless think it feasible in large towns, where the rich might subscribe for the religious instruction of the poor. Alas! they know little of the thick darkness that spreads over the streets and alleys of our large towns. The parish of Lambeth, a few years since, contained not more than one church and three or four small proprietary chapels, while dissenting chapels of every denomination were still more scantily found there; yet the inhabitants of the parish amounted at that time to upwards of 50,000. Were the parish church and the chapels of the Establishment existing there an *impediment* to the spread of the Gospel among that mass of people? Who shall dare to say so? But if any one, in the face of the fact which has just been stated, and in opposition to authentic reports to the same effect from various other quarters, should still contend that a voluntary system is sufficient for the spread and maintenance of religion, we would ask, what kind of religion? wherein would it differ, among the many, from deplorable fanaticism?

For the preservation of the Church Establishment, all men, whether they belong to it or not, could they perceive their true interest, would be strenuous; but how inadequate are its provisions for the needs of the country! and how much is it to be regretted that, while its zealous friends yield to alarms on account of the hostility of dissent, they should so much overrate the danger to be apprehended from that quarter, and almost overlook the fact that hundreds of thousands of our fellow-countrymen, though formally and nominally of the Church of England, never enter her places of worship, neither have they communication with her ministers! This deplorable state of things was partly produced by a decay of zeal among the rich and influential, and partly by a want of due expansive power in the constitution of the Establishment as regulated by law. Private benefactors, in their efforts to build and endow churches, have been frustrated or too much impeded by legal obstacles; these, where they are unreasonable or unfitted for the times, ought to be removed; and, keeping clear of intolerance and injustice, means should be used to render the presence and powers of the church commensurate with the wants of a shifting and still-increasing population.

This cannot be affected, unless the English Government vindicate the truth that, as her church exists for the benefit of all (though not in equal degree), whether of her communion or not, all should be made to contribute to its support. If this ground be abandoned, cause will be given to fear that a moral wound may be inflicted upon the heart of the English people, for which a remedy cannot be speedily provided by the utmost efforts which the members of the Church will themselves be able to make.

But let the friends of the church be of good courage. Powers are at work, by which, under Divine Providence, she may be strengthened and the sphere of her usefulness extended; not by alterations in her Liturgy, accommodated to this or that demand of finical taste, nor by cutting off this or that from her articles or Canons, to which the scrupulous or the overweening may object. Covert schism, and open nonconformity, would survive after alterations, however promising in the eyes of those

[137]

whose subtilty had been exercised in making them. Latitudinarianism is the parhelion of liberty of conscience, and will ever successfully lay claim to a divided worship. Among Presbyterians, Socinians, Baptists, and Independents, there will always be found numbers who will tire of their several creeds, and some will come over to the Church. Conventicles may disappear, congregations in each denomination may fall into decay or be broken up, but the conquests which the National Church ought chiefly to aim at, lie among the thousands and tens of thousands of the unhappy outcasts who grow up with no religion at all. The wants of these cannot but be feelingly remembered. Whatever may be the disposition of the new constituencies under the reformed parliament, and the course which the men of their choice may be inclined or compelled to follow, it may be confidently hoped that individuals, acting in their private capacities, will endeavour to make up for the deficiencies of the legislature. Is it too much to expect that proprietors of large estates, where the inhabitants are without religious instruction, or where it is sparingly supplied, will deem it their duty to take part in this good work; and that thriving manufacturers and merchants will, in their several neighbourhoods, be sensible of the like obligation, and act upon it with generous rivalry?

Moreover, the force of public opinion is rapidly increasing, and some may bend to it, who are not so happy as to be swayed by a higher motive; especially they who derive large incomes from lay-impropriations in tracts of country where ministers are few and meagrely provided for. A claim still stronger may be acknowledged by those who, round their superb habitations, or elsewhere, walk over vast estates which were lavished upon their ancestors by royal favouritism or purchased at insignificant prices after church-spoliation; such proprietors, though not conscience-stricken (there is no call for that), may be prompted to make a return for which their tenantry and dependents will learn to bless their names. An impulse has been given; an accession of means from these several sources, co-operating with a *well*-considered change in the distribution of some parts of the property at present possessed by the church, a change scrupulously founded upon due respect to law and justice, will, we trust, bring about so much of what her friends desire, that the rest may be calmly waited for, with thankfulness for what shall have been obtained.

Let it not be thought unbecoming in a layman to have treated at length a subject with which the clergy are more intimately conversant. All may, without impropriety, speak of what deeply concerns all; nor need an apology be offered for going over ground which has been trod before so ably and so often: without pretending, however, to anything of novelty, either in matter or manner, something may have been offered to view which will save the writer from the imputation of having little to recommend his labour but goodness of intention.

POSTSCRIPT

It was with reference to thoughts and feelings expressed in verse, that I entered upon the above notices, and with verse I will conclude. The passage is extracted from my MSS. written above thirty years ago: it turns upon the individual dignity which humbleness of social condition does not preclude, but frequently promotes. It has no direct bearing upon clubs for the discussion of public affairs, nor upon political or trade-unions; but if a single workman — who, being a member of one of those clubs, runs the risk of becoming an agitator, or who, being enrolled in a union, must be left without a will of his own, and therefore a slave — should read these lines, and be touched by them, I should indeed rejoice, and little would I care for losing credit as a poet with intemperate critics, who think differently from me upon political philosophy or public measures, if the sober-minded admit that, in general views, my affections have been moved, and my imagination exercised, under and *for* the guidance of reason.

> "Here might I pause, and bend in reverence\
> To Nature, and the power of human minds;
> To men as they are men within themselves.
> How oft high service is performed within,
> When all the external man is rude in show;
> Not like a temple rich with pomp and gold,
> But a mere mountain chapel that protects
> Its simple worshippers from sun and shower!
> Of these, said I, shall be my song; of these,
> If future years mature me for the task,
> Will I record the praises, making verse
> Deal boldly with substantial things — in truth

POSTSCRIPT

And sanctity of passion, speak of these,
That justice may be done, obeisance paid
Where it is due. Thus haply shall I teach,
Inspire, through unadulterated ears
Pour rapture, tenderness, and hope; my theme
No other than the very heart of man,
As found among the best of those who live,
Not unexalted by religious faith,
Nor uninformed by books, good books, though few,
In Nature's presence: thence may I select
Sorrow that is not sorrow, but delight,
And miserable love that is not pain
To hear of, for the glory that rebounds
Therefrom to human kind, and what we are.
Be mine to follow with no timid step
Where knowledge leads me; it shall be my pride
That I have dared to tread this holy ground,
Speaking no dream, but things oracular,
Matter not lightly to be heard by those
Who to the letter of the outward promise
Do read the invisible soul; by men adroit
In speech, and for communion with the world
Accomplished, minds whose faculties are then
Most active when they are most eloquent,
And elevated most when most admired.
Men may be found of other mould than these;
Who are their own upholders, to themselves
Encouragement and energy, and will;
Expressing liveliest thoughts in lively words
As native passion dictates. Others, too,
There are, among the walks of homely life,
Still higher, men for contemplation framed;
Shy, and unpractised in the strife of phrase;
Meek men, whose very souls perhaps would sink
Beneath them, summoned to such intercourse.
Theirs is the language of the heavens, the power,

POSTSCRIPT

The thought, the image, and the silent joy:
Words are but under-agents in their souls;
When they are grasping with their greatest strength
They do not breathe among them; this I speak
In gratitude to God, who feeds our hearts
For his own service, knoweth, loveth us,
When we are unregarded by the world."

NOTES

VOLUME I

1. These lines are only applicable to the middle part of that lake.

2. In the beginning of the winter, these mountains are frequented by woodcocks.

3. The word *intake* is local, and signifies a mountain enclosure.

4. Ghyll is also, I believe, a term confined to this country: *ghyll* and *dingle* have the same meaning.

5. The reader who has made a tour of this country, will recognise, in this description, the features which characterise the lower waterfall in the grounds of Rydal.

6. "Vivid rings of green." — Greenwood's *Poems on Shooting*.

7. "Dolcemente feroce." — TASSO.

In this description of the cock, I remembered a spirited one of the same animal in *L'Agriculture, ou Les Georgiques François*, of M. Bossuet.

8. From Thomson.

9. See a description of an appearance of this kind in Clark's *Survey of the Lakes*, accompanied by vouchers of its veracity, that may amuse the reader.

10. Collins's "Ode on the Death of Thomson," the

last written, I believe, of the poems which were published during his lifetime. This Ode is also alluded to in the next Stanza.

11. The lyre of Memnon is reported to have emitted melancholy or cheerful tones, as it was touched by the sun's evening or morning rays.

12. Alluding to the crosses seen on the tops of the spiry rocks of the Chartreuse, which have every appearance of being inaccessible.

13. Names of rivers at the Chartreuse.

14. Name of one of the valleys of the Chartreuse.

15. The river along whose banks you descend in crossing the Alps by the Simplon Pass.

16. Most of the bridges among the Alps are of wood, and covered: these bridges have a heavy appearance, and rather injure the effect of the Scenery in some places.

17. The Catholic religion prevails here: these cells are, as is well known, very common in the Catholic countries, planted, like the Roman tombs, along the roadside.

18. Crosses, commemorative of the deaths of travellers by the fall of snow, and other accidents, are very common along this dreadful road.

19. The houses in the more retired Swiss valleys are all built of wood.

20. For most of the images in the next sixteen verses, I am indebted to M. Raymond's interesting observations annexed to his translation of Coxe's *Tour in Switzerland.*

21. The people of this Canton are supposed to be of a more melancholy disposition than the other inhabitants of the Alps; this, if true, may proceed from their being more secluded.

22. This picture is from the middle region of the Alps. *Chalets* are summer huts for the Swiss herdsmen.

23. Sugh, a Scotch word expressive of the sound of the wind through the trees.

24. Alluding to several battles which the Swiss in very small numbers have gained over their oppressors, the house of Austria; and in particular to one fought at Naeffels, near Glarus, where three hundred and fifty men are said to have defeated an army of between fifteen and twenty thousand Austrians. Scattered over the valley are to be found eleven stones, with this inscription, 1388, the year the battle was fought, marking out, as I was told upon the spot, the several places where the Austrians, attempting to make a stand, were repulsed anew.

25. As Schreck-Horn, the pike of terror; Wetter-Horn, the pike of storms, etc., etc.

26. The well-known effect of the famous air called in French "Ranz des Vaches," upon the Swiss troops.

27. This shrine is resorted to, from a hope of relief, by multitudes from every corner of the Catholic world, labouring under mental or bodily afflictions.

28. Rude fountains built and covered with sheds for the accommodation of the Pilgrims, in their ascent of the mountain.

29. An insect so called, which emits a short, melancholy cry, heard at the close of the summer evenings, on the banks of the Loire.

30. The duties upon many parts of the French rivers were so exorbitant that the poorer people, deprived of the benefit of water carriage, were obliged to transport their goods by land.

31. From a short MS. poem read to me when an undergraduate, by my schoolfellow and friend, Charles Farish, long since deceased. The verses were by a brother of his, a man of promising genius, who died young.

32. This Dramatic Piece, as noticed in its title-page, was composed in 1795–96. It lay nearly from that time till within the last two or three months unregarded among my papers, without being mentioned even to my most intimate friends. Having, however, impressions upon my mind which made me unwilling to destroy the MS., I determined to undertake the responsibility of publishing it during my own life, rather than impose upon my successors the task of deciding its fate. Accordingly it has been revised with some care; but, as it was at first written, and is now published, without any view to its exhibition upon the stage, not the slightest alteration has been made in the conduct of the story, or the composition of the characters; above all, in respect to the two leading Persons of the Drama, I felt no inducement to make any change. The study of human nature suggests this awful truth: that as in the trials to which life subjects us, sin and crime are apt

to start from their very opposite qualities, so are there no limits to the hardening of the heart, and the perversion of the understanding to which they may carry their slaves. During my long residence in France, while the Revolution was rapidly advancing to its extreme of wickedness, I had frequent opportunities of being an eye-witness of this process, and it was while that knowledge was fresh upon my memory that the Tragedy of "The Borderers" was composed.

VOLUME II

1. The river is not affected by the tides a few miles above Tintern.

2. This line has a close resemblance to an admirable line of Young's, the exact expression of which I do not recollect.

3. In the dialect of the North, a hawker of earthenware is thus designated.

4.   "Not mine own fears, nor the prophetic Soul
        Of the wide world dreaming on things to come."
                                    Shakespeare's Sonnets.

5. This description of the Calenture is sketched from an imperfect recollection of an admirable one in prose, by Mr. Gilbert, author of the *Hurricane*.

6. The Great Gavel, so called, I imagine, from its resemblance to the gable end of a house, is one of the highest of the Cumberland Mountains. It stands at the head of the several vales of Ennerdale, Wastdale, and

Borrowdale. The Leeza is a river which flows into the lake of Ennerdale: on issuing from the Lake, it changes its name, and is called the End, Eyne, or Enna. It falls into the Sea a little below Egremont.

7. Clipping is the word used in the North of England for shearing.

8. *Ghyll*, in the dialect of Cumberland and Westmoreland, is a short, and, for the most part, a steep narrow valley, with a stream running through it. *Force* is the word universally employed in these dialects for waterfall.

9. In several parts of the North of England, when a funeral takes place, a basin full of sprigs of boxwood is placed at the door of the house from which the coffin is taken up, and each person who attends the funeral ordinarily takes a sprig of this boxwood, and throws it into the grave of the deceased.

10. Great How is a single and conspicuous hill, which rises towards the foot of Thirlmere, on the western side of the beautiful dale of Legberthwaite, along the highroad between Keswick and Ambleside.

11. The Kirtle is a river in the southern part of Scotland, on the banks of which the events here related took place.

VOLUME III

1. Dominique de Gourgues, a French gentleman who went in 1568 to Florida to avenge the massacre of the French by the Spaniards there.

2. These lines have been printed before. See vol. ii, pp. 157–159.

3. The late Rev. John Fleming, of Rayrigg, Windermere.

4. Hawkshead.

5. See vol. ii, pp. 160, 161.

6. See vol. ii, p. 156.

7. The City of Goslar, in Lower Saxony.

8. See p. 132.

9. These lines are from a descriptive poem — "Malvern Hills" — by one of Mr. Wordsworth's oldest friends, Mr. Joseph Cottle.

10. See vol. i, pp. 8, 9.

11. From Milton, *Paradise Lost*, xi, 204.

12. See "Vaudracour and Julia," vol. iv, p. 267.

13. See vol. iv, pp. 317, 318.

14. *Theocrit. Idyll.*, vii, 78.

VOLUME IV

1. *With such a master*, etc. From a Bodleian, as are also Stanzas xliv and xlv, which are necessary to complete the sense.

2. See *Paradise Lost*, book xi, where Adam points out to Eve the ominous sign of the Eagle chasing "two birds of gayest plume," and the gentle Hart and Hind pursued by their enemy.

3. Common pilewort.

4. (See Dedication to "Descriptive Sketches.")

This excellent Person, one of my earliest and dearest friends, died in the year 1835. We were undergraduates together of the same year, at the same college; and companions in many a delightful ramble through his own romantic Country of North Wales. Much of the latter part of his life he passed in comparative solitude, which I know was often cheered by remembrance of our youthful adventures, and of the beautiful regions which, at home and abroad, we had visited together. Our long friendship was never subject to a moment's interrup͟ion, — and, while revising these volumes for the last time, I have been so often reminded of my loss, with a not unpleasing sadness, that I trust the Reader will excuse this passing mention of a Man who well deserves from me something more than so brief a notice. Let me only add, that during the middle part of his life he resided many years (as Incumbent of the Living) at a Parsonage in Oxfordshire, which is the subject of the sonnet entitled "A Parsonage in Oxfordshire," vol. ͟ ͟ ͟ entitled "A Parsonage in Oxfordshire," vii, p. 242.

5. Fourteenth of ͟ ͟ ͟ 120. ͟and a succeeding sonnet on the same subject, let me be understood as a Poet availing himself of the situation which the King of Sweden occupied, and of the principles AVOWED IN HIS MANIFESTOES; as laying hold of these advantages for the purpose of embodying moral truths. This remark might, perhaps, as well have been suppressed; for to those who may be in sympathy with the course of these Poems, it will be super-

fluous, and will, I fear, be thrown away upon that other class, whose besotted admiration of the intoxicated despot hereafter placed in contrast with him, is the most melancholy evidence of degradation in British feeling and intellect which the times have furnished.

7. This Poem, and two others to the same flower, were written in the year 1802; which is mentioned, because in some of the ideas, though not in the manner in which those ideas are connected, and likewise even in some of the expressions, there is a resemblance to passages in a poem (lately published) of Mr. Montgomery's, entitled, "A Field Flower." This being said, Mr. Montgomery will not think any apology due to him; I cannot, however, help addressing him in the words of the Father of English Poets: —

> "Though it happe me to rehersin —
> That ye han in your freshe songis saied,
> Forberith me, and beth not ill apaied,
> Sith that ye se I doe it in the honour
> Of Love, and eke in service of the Flour."

1807.

8. His muse.

9. See, in Chaucer and the elder Poets, the honours formerly paid to the flower.

10. Written at Grasmere. In no part of England, or of Europe, have I ever seen a yew-tree at all approaching this in magnitude.

11. The following is extracted from the journal of my fellow-traveller, to which, as persons acquainted with my poems will know, I have been obliged on other occasions:

"DUMFRIES, August 1803.

"On our way to the churchyard where Burns is buried, we were accompanied by a bookseller, who showed us the outside of Burns's house, where he had lived the last three years of his life, and where he died. It has a mean appearance, and is in a bye situation; the front whitewashed; dirty about the doors, as most Scotch houses are; flowering plants in the window. Went to visit his grave; he lies in a corner of the churchyard, and his second son, Francis Wallace, beside him. There is no stone to mark the spot; but a hundred guineas have been collected to be expended upon some sort of monument. 'There,' said the bookseller, pointing to a pompous monument, 'lies Mr.' — (I have forgotten the name) — 'a remarkably clever man; he was an attorney, and scarcely ever lost a cause he undertook. Burns made many a lampoon upon him, and there they rest as you see.' We looked at Burns's grave with melancholy and painful reflections, repeating to each other his own poet's epitaph: —

'Is there a man,' etc.

"The churchyard is full of grave-stones and expensive monuments, in all sorts of fantastic shapes, obelisk-wise, pillar-wise, etc. When our guide had left us we turned again to Burns's grave, and afterwards went to his house, wishing to enquire after Mrs. Burns, who was gone to spend some time by the seashore with her children. We spoke to the maid-servant at the door, who invited us forward, and we sate down in the parlour. The

walls were coloured with a blue wash; on one side of the
fire was a mahogany desk; opposite the window a clock,
which Burns mentions, in one of his letters, having received as a present. The house was cleanly and neat
in the inside, the stairs of stone scoured white, the
kitchen on the right side of the passage, the parlour on
the left. In the room above the parlour the poet died,
and his son, very lately, in the same room. The servant
told us she had lived four years with Mrs. Burns, who
was now in great sorrow for the death of Wallace. She
said that Mrs. B.'s youngest son was now at Christ's
Hospital. We were glad to leave Dumfries, where we
could think of little but poor Burns, and his moving
about on that unpoetic ground. In our road to Brown-
hill, the next stage, we passed Ellisland, at a little distance on our right — his farm-house. Our pleasure in
looking round would have been still greater, if the road
had led us nearer the spot.

.   .   .   .

"I cannot take leave of this country which we passed
through to-day, without mentioning that we saw the
Cumberland mountains within half a mile of Ellisland,
Burns's house, the last view we had of them. Drayton
has prettily described the connection which this neighbourhood has with ours, when he makes Skiddaw say, —

'Scruffel, from the sky
That Annandale doth crown, with a most amorous eye
Salutes me every day, or at my pride looks grim,
Oft threatening me with clouds, as I oft threaten him.'

"These lines came to my brother's memory, as well as the Cumberland saying, —

> 'If Skiddaw hath a cap
> Scruffel was well of that.'

"We talked of Burns, and of the prospect he must have had, perhaps from his own door, of Skiddaw and his companions; indulging ourselves in the fancy that we might have been personally known to each other, and he have looked upon those objects with more pleasure for our sakes."

12. The tradition is that the Castle was built by a Lady during the absence of her Lord in Palestine.

13. See Hamilton's Ballad as above [in headnote to the poem].

14. It is recorded in Dampier's *Voyages*, that a boy, son of the captain of a Man-of-War, seated himself in a Turtle-Shell, and floated in it from the shore to his father's ship, which lay at anchor at the distance of half a mile. In deference to the opinion of a Friend, I have substituted such a shell for the less elegant vessel in which my blind Voyager did actually entrust himself to the dangerous current of Loch Leven, as was related to me by an eye-witness.

15. With this picture, which was taken from real life, compare the imaginative one of "The Reverie of Poor Susan," vol. i, p. 218; and see (to make up the deficiencies of this class) "The Excursion," *passim*.

16. Town-End, 1804. The two best lines in it are by Mary.

17. The story of this poem is from the German of Frederica Brun.

18. A small Mere or Lake, mostly high up in the mountains.

19. *Moss Campion (Silene acaulis).* This most beautiful plant is scarce in England, though it is found in great abundance upon the mountains of Scotland. The first specimen I ever saw of it, in its native bed, was singularly fine, the tuft or cushion being at least eight inches in diameter, and the root proportionably thick. I have only met with it in two places among our mountains, in both of which I have since sought for it in vain.

Botanists will not, I hope, take it ill, if I caution them against carrying off, inconsiderately, rare and beautiful plants. This has often been done, particularly from Ingleborough, and other mountains in Yorkshire, till the species have totally disappeared, to the great regret of lovers of Nature living near the places where they grew.

20. Several years after the event that forms the subject of the Poem, in company with my friend, the late Mr. Coleridge, I happened to fall in with the person to whom the name of Benjamin is given. Upon our expressing regret that we had not, for a long time, seen upon the road either him or his wagon, he said, "They could not do without me; and as to the man who was put in my place, no good could come out of him; he was a man of no *ideas.*"

The fact of my discarded hero's getting the horses out of a great difficulty with a word, as related in the Poem, was told me by an eye-witness.

21. When the Poem was first written the note of the bird was thus described: —

> "The Night-hawk is singing his frog-like tune,
> Twirling his watchman's rattle about —"

but from unwillingness to startle the reader at the outset by so bold a mode of expression, the passage was altered as it now stands.

22. This rude piece of self-taught art (such is the progress of refinement) has been supplanted by a professional production.

23. A mountain of Grasmere, the broken summit of which presents two figures, full as distinctly shaped as that of the famous Cobbler near Arroquhar in Scotland.

24. A term well known in the North of England, as applied to rural festivals where young persons meet in the evening for the purpose of dancing.

25. At the close of each strathspey, or jig, a particular note from the fiddle summons the rustic to the agreeable duty of saluting his partner.

26. After the line, "Can any mortal clog come to her," followed in the MS. an incident which has been kept back. Part of the suppressed verses shall here be given as a gratification of private feeling, which the well-disposed reader will find no difficulty in excusing. They are now printed for the first time.

"Can any mortal clog come to her?
It can   .   .   .   .

.   .   .   .

But Benjamin, in his vexation,
Possesses inward consolation;
He knows his ground, and hopes to find
A spot with all things to his mind,
An upright mural block of stone,
Moist with pure water trickling down.
A slender spring ; but kind to man
It is, a true Samaritan;
Close to the highway, pouring out
Its offering from a chink or spout ;
Whence all, howe'er athirst, or drooping
With toil, may drink, and without stooping.
    Cries Benjamin, 'Where is it, where?
Voice it hath none, but must be near.'
— A star, declining towards the west,
Upon the watery surface threw
Its image tremulously imprest,
That just marked out the object and withdrew:
Right welcome service!   .   .   .   .   .

.   .   .   .

ROCK OF NAMES!

Light is the strain, but not unjust
To Thee, and thy memorial trust
That once seemed only to express
Love that was love in idleness;
Tokens, as year hath followed year
How changed, alas, in character!
For they were graven on thy smooth breast
By hands of those my soul loved best;
Meek women, men as true and brave
As ever went to a hopeful grave:
Their hands and mine, when side by side
With kindred zeal and mutual pride,

> We worked until the Initials took
> Shapes that defied a scornful look. —
> Long as for us a genial feeling
> Survives, or one in need of healing,
> The power, dear Rock, around thee cast,
> Thy monumental power, shall last
> For me and mine! O thought of pain,
> That would impair it or profane!
> Take all in kindness then, as said
> With a staid heart but playful head;
> And fail not Thou, loved Rock! to keep
> Thy charge when we are laid asleep."

27. The crag of the ewe lamb.

28. This and the Extract, vol. ii, p. 157, and the first Piece of this Class, are from the [then] unpublished Poem of which some account is given in the Preface to THE EXCURSION.

VOLUME V

1. This story is a Cumberland tradition. I have heard it also related of the Hall of Hutton John, an ancient residence of the Hudlestons in a sequestered valley upon the river Dacor.

2. "Importuna e grave salma." — MICHAEL ANGELO.

3. "Danger which they fear, and honour which they understand not." — Words in Lord Brooke's Life of Sir P. Sidney.

4. Mrs. Wordsworth has a strong impression that "The Mother's Return" was written at Coleorton, where Miss Wordsworth was then staying with the children, during the absence of the former.

5. Henry Lord Clifford, etc., who is the subject of this Poem, was the son of John Lord Clifford, who was slain at Towton Field, which John Lord Clifford, as is known to the reader of English history, was the person who after the battle of Wakefield slew, in the pursuit, the young Earl of Rutland, son of the Duke of York, who had fallen in the battle, "in part of revenge" (say the Authors of the *History of Cumberland and Westmoreland*); "for the Earl's Father had slain his." A deed which worthily blemished the author (saith Speed); but who, as he adds, "dare promise any thing temperate of himself in the heat of martial fury? chiefly, when it was resolved not to leave any branch of the York line standing; for so one maketh this Lord to speak." This, no doubt, I would observe by the bye, was an action sufficiently in the vindictive spirit of the times, and yet not altogether so bad as represented; "for the Earl was no child, as some writers would have him, but able to bear arms, being sixteen or seventeen years of age, as is evident from this (say the Memoirs of the Countess of Pembroke, who was laudably anxious to wipe away, as far as could be, this stigma from the illustrious name to which she was born), that he was the next Child to King Edward the Fourth, which his mother had by Richard Duke of York, and that King was then eighteen years of age: and for the small distance betwixt her children, see Austin Vincent, in his *Book of Nobility*, p. 622, where he writes of them all." It may further be observed, that Lord Clifford, who was

then himself only twenty-five years of age, had been a leading man and commander of two or three years together in the army of Lancaster, before this time; and, therefore, would be less likely to think that the Earl of Rutland might be entitled to mercy from his youth. — But, independent of this act, at best a cruel and savage one, the Family of Clifford had done enough to draw upon them the vehement hatred of the House of York: so that after the Battle of Towton there was no hope for them but in flight and concealment. Henry, the subject of the Poem, was deprived of his estate and honours during the space of twenty-four years; all which time he lived as a shepherd in Yorkshire, or in Cumberland, where the estate of his Father-in-law (Sir Lancelot Threlkeld) lay. He was restored to his estate and honours in the first year of Henry the Seventh. It is recorded that, "when called to Parliament, he behaved nobly and wisely; but otherwise came seldom to London or the Court; and rather delighted to live in the country, where he repaired several of his Castles, which had gone to decay during the late troubles." Thus far is chiefly collected from Nicholson and Burn; and I can add, from my own knowledge, that there is a tradition current in the village of Threlkeld and its neighbourhood, his principal retreat, that in the course of his shepherd-life he had acquired great astronomical knowledge. I cannot conclude this note without adding a word upon the subject of those numerous and noble feudal Edi-

St. Oswald's Church, Grasmere

fices, spoken of in the Poem, the ruins of some of which are, at this day, so great an ornament to that interesting country. The Cliffords had always been distinguished for an honourable pride in these Castles; and we have seen that, after the wars of York and Lancaster, they were rebuilt; in the civil wars of Charles the First they were again laid waste, and again restored almost to their former magnificence by the celebrated Lady Anne Clifford, Countess of Pembroke, etc. Not more than twenty-five years after this was done, when the estates of Clifford had passed into the Family of Tufton, three of these Castles, namely, Brough, Brougham, and Pendragon, were demolished, and the timber and other materials sold by Thomas Earl of Thanet. We will hope that, when this order was issued, the Earl had not consulted the text of Isaiah, 58th chap., 12th verse, to which the inscription placed over the gate of Pendragon Castle by the Countess of Pembroke (I believe his Grandmother), at the time she repaired that structure, refers the reader: *"And they that shall be of thee shall build the old waste places: thou shalt raise up the foundations of many generations; and thou shalt be called, The repairer of the breach, The restorer of paths to dwell in."* The Earl of Thanet, the present possessor of the Estates, with a due respect for the memory of his ancestors, and a proper sense of the value and beauty of these remains of antiquity, has (I am told) given orders that they shall be preserved from all depredations.

6. This line is from "The Battle of Bosworth Field,"

by Sir John Beaumont (brother to the Dramatist), whose poems are written with much spirit, elegance, and harmony, and have deservedly been reprinted lately in Chalmers's Collection of English Poets.

7. It is imagined by the people of the country that there are two immortal Fish, inhabitants of this Tarn, which lies in the mountains not far from Threlkeld. — Blencathara, mentioned before, is the old and proper name of the mountain vulgarly called Saddleback.

8. The martial character of the Cliffords is well known to the readers of English history; but it may not be improper here to say, by way of comment on these lines and what follows, that besides several others who perished in the same manner, the four immediate Progenitors of the Person in whose hearing this is supposed to be spoken all died in the Field.

9. The Poem of "The White Doe of Rylstone" is founded on a local tradition, and on the Ballad in Percy's Collection, entitled "The Rising of the North." The tradition is as follows: "About this time," not long after the Dissolution, "a White Doe," say the aged people of the neighbourhood, "long continued to make a weekly pilgrimage from Rylstone over the fells of Bolton, and was constantly found in the Abbey Churchyard during divine service; after the close of which she returned home as regularly as the rest of the congregation." — DR. WHITAKER's *History of the Deanery of Craven.*

Rylstone was the property and residence of the

Nortons, distinguished in that ill-advised and unfortunate Insurrection; which led me to connect with this tradition the principal circumstances of their fate, as recorded in the Ballad.

"Bolton Priory," says Dr. Whitaker in his excellent book, *The History and Antiquities of the Deanery of Craven*, "stands upon a beautiful curvature of the Wharf, on a level sufficiently elevated to protect it from inundations, and low enough for every purpose of picturesque effect.

"Opposite to the East window of the Priory Church, the river washes the foot of a rock nearly perpendicular, and of the richest purple, where several of the mineral beds, which break out instead of maintaining their usual inclination to the horizon, are twisted by some inconceivable process into undulating and spiral lines. To the South all is soft and delicious; the eye reposes upon a few rich pastures, a moderate reach of the river, sufficiently tranquil to form a mirror to the sun, and the bounding hills beyond, neither too near nor too lofty to exclude, even in winter, any portion of his rays.

"But after all, the glories of Bolton are on the North. Whatever the most fastidious taste could require to constitute a perfect landscape, is not only found here, but in its proper place. In front, and immediately under the eye, is a smooth expanse of park-like enclosure, spotted with native elm, ash, etc., of the finest growth: on the right a skirting oak wood, with jutting points of grey rock; on the left a rising copse. Still forward are seen the aged grooves of Bolton Park, the growth of centuries; and farther yet, the barren and rocky distances of Simon-seat and Barden Fell contrasted with the warmth, fertility, and luxuriant foliage of the valley below.

"About half a mile above Bolton the valley closes, and either side of the Wharf is overhung by solemn woods, from which huge perpendicular masses of grey rock jut out at intervals.

"This sequestered scene was almost inaccessible till of late, that ridings have been cut on both sides of the river, and the most interesting points laid open by judicious thinnings in the woods. Here a tributary stream rushes from a waterfall, and bursts through a woody glen to mingle its waters with the Wharf: there the Wharf itself is nearly lost in a deep cleft in the rock, and next becomes a horned flood enclosing a woody island — sometimes it reposes for a moment, and then resumes its native character, lively, irregular, and impetuous.

"The cleft mentioned above is the tremendous Strid. This chasm, being incapable of receiving the winter floods, has formed on either side a broad strand of naked gritstone full of rock-basins, or 'pots of the Linn,' which bear witness to the restless impetuosity of so many Northern torrents. But, if here Wharf is lost to the eye, it amply repays another sense by its deep and solemn roar, like 'the Voice of the angry Spirit of

the Waters,' heard far above and beneath, amidst the
silence of the surrounding woods.

"The terminating object of the landscape is the remains of Barden Tower, interesting from their form
and situation, and still more so from the recollections
which they excite."

10. This and the five lines that follow were either
read or recited by me, more than thirty years since, to
the late Mr. Hazlitt, who quoted some expressions in
them (imperfectly remembered) in a work of his published several years ago.

11. It is to be regretted that at the present day
Bolton Abbey wants this ornament: but the Poem, according to the imagination of the Poet, is composed in
Queen Elizabeth's time. "Formerly," says Dr. Whitaker, "over the Transept was a tower. This is proved not
only from the mention of bells at the Dissolution, when
they could have had no other place, but from the pointed
roof of the choir, which must have terminated west-
ward, in some building of superior height to the ridge."

12. "The Nave of the Church having been reserved
at the Dissolution for the use of the Saxon Cure, is still
a parochial Chapel: and, at this day, is as well kept
as the neatest English Cathedral."

13. "At a small distance from the great gateway
stood the Prior's Oak, which was felled about the year
1720, and sold for 70*l.* According to the price of wood
at that time, it could scarcely have contained less than
1400 feet of timber."

14. The detail of this tradition may be found in Dr. Whitaker's book, and in a Poem of this Collection, "The Force of Prayer."

15. At the East end of the North aisle of Bolton Priory Church, is a chantry belonging to Bethmesly Hall, and a vault where, according to tradition, the Claphams (who inherited this estate, by the female line, from the Mauleverers) were interred upright. John de Clapham, of whom this ferocious act is recorded, was a man of great note in his time: he was a vehement partisan of the house of Lancaster, in whom the spirit of his chieftains, the Cliffords, seemed to survive.

16. Among these Poems will be found one entitled, "Song at the Feast of Brougham Castle, upon the Restoration of Lord Clifford, the Shepherd, to the Estates and Honours of his Ancestors." To that Poem is annexed an account of this personage, chiefly extracted from Burn and Nicholson's *History of Cumberland and Westmoreland*. It gives me pleasure to add these further particulars concerning him, from Dr. Whitaker, who says he "retired to the solitude of Barden, where he seems to have enlarged the tower out of a common keeper's lodge, and where he found a retreat equally favourable to taste, to instruction, and to devotion. The narrow limits of his residence show that he had learned to despise the pomp of greatness, and that a small train of servants could suffice him, who had lived to the age of thirty a servant himself. I think

this nobleman resided here almost entirely when in Yorkshire, for all his charters which I have seen are dated at Barden.

"His early habits, and the want of those artificial measures of time which even shepherds now possess, had given him a turn for observing the motions of the heavenly bodies; and, having purchased such an apparatus as could then be procured, he amused and informed himself by those pursuits, with the aid of the Canons of Bolton, some of whom are said to have been well versed in what was then known of the science.

"I suspect this nobleman to have been sometimes occupied in a more visionary pursuit, and probably in the same company.

"For, from the family evidences, I have met with two MSS. on the subject of Alchemy, which, from the character, spelling, etc., may almost certainly be referred to the reign of Henry the Seventh. If these were originally deposited with the MSS. of the Cliffords, it might have been for the use of this nobleman. If they were brought from Bolton at the Dissolution, they must have been the work of those Canons whom he almost exclusively conversed with.

"In these peaceful employments Lord Clifford spent the whole reign of Henry the Seventh, and the first years of his son. But in the year 1513, when almost sixty years old, he was appointed to a principal command over the army which fought at Flodden, and showed that the military genius of the family had neither been chilled in him by age, nor extinguished by habits of peace.

"He survived the battle of Flodden ten years, and died April 23, 1523, aged about 70. I shall endeavour to appropriate to him a tomb, vault, and chantry, in the choir of the church of Bolton, as I should be sorry to believe that he was deposited, when dead, at a distance from the place which in his lifetime he loved so well.

"By his last will he appointed his body to be interred at Shap, if he died in Westmoreland; or at Bolton, if he died in Yorkshire."

With respect to the Canons of Bolton, Dr. Whitaker shows from MSS. that not only alchemy but astronomy was a favourite pursuit with them.

17. See the Old Ballad, — "The Rising of the North."

18. Brancepeth Castle stands near the river Were, a few miles from the city of Durham. It formerly belonged to the Nevilles, Earls of Westmoreland. See Dr. Percy's account.

19. From the old ballad.

20. From the old ballad.

21. See the Historians for the account of this memorable battle, usually denominated the Battle of the Standard.

22. "In the night before the battle of Durham was strucken and begun, the 17th day of October, *anno* 1346, there did appear to John Fosser, then Prior of the abbey of Durham, a Vision, commanding him to

take the holy Corporax-cloth, wherewith St. Cuthbert did cover the chalice when he used to say mass, and to put the same holy relique like to a banner-cloth upon the point of a spear, and the next morning to go and repair to a place on the west side of the city of Durham, called the Red Hills, where the Maid's Bower wont to be, and there to remain and abide till the end of the battle. To which vision the Prior obeying, and taking the same for a revelation of God's grace and mercy by the mediation of Holy St. Cuthbert, did accordingly the next morning, with the monks of the said abbey, repair to the said Red Hills, and there most devoutly humbling and prostrating themselves in prayer for the victory in the said battle: (a great multitude of the Scots running and pressing by them, with intention to have spoiled them, yet had no power to commit any violence under such holy persons, so occupied in prayer, being protected and defended by the mighty Providence of Almighty God, and by the mediation of Holy St. Cuthbert, and the presence of the holy relique.)   And, after many conflicts and warlike exploits there had and done between the English men and the King of Scots and his company, the said battle ended, and the victory was obtained, to the great overthrow and confusion of the Scots, their enemies: And then the said Prior and monks accompanied with Ralph Lord Nevil, and John Nevil his son, and the Lord Percy, and many other nobles of England, returned home and went to the abbey church, there

joining in hearty prayer and thanksgiving to God
and Holy St. Cuthbert for the victory achieved that
day."

This battle was afterwards called the Battle of
Neville's Cross from the following circumstance: —

"On the west side of the city of Durham, where
two roads pass each other, a most notable, famous, and
goodly cross of stone-work was erected and set up to
the honour of God for the victory there obtained in the
field of battle, and known by the name of Nevil's Cross,
and built at the sole cost of the Lord Ralph Nevil, one
of the most excellent and chief persons in the said
battle." The Relique of St. Cuthbert afterwards became of great importance in military events. For soon
after this battle, says the same author, "The Prior
caused a goodly and sumptuous banner to be made"
(which is then described at great length), "and in the
midst of the same banner-cloth was the said holy relique
and corporax-cloth enclosed, etc., and so sumptuously
finished, and absolutely perfected, this banner was dedicated to Holy St. Cuthbert, of intent and purpose
that for the future it should be carried to any battle,
as occasion should serve; and was never carried and
showed at any battle but by the especial grace of God
Almighty, and the mediation of Holy St. Cuthbert, it
brought home victory; which banner-cloth, after the
dissolution of the abbey, fell into the possession of
Dean WHITTINGHAM, whose wife, called KATHARINE,
being a French woman (as is most credibly reported

by eye-witnesses), did most injuriously burn the same in her fire, to the open contempt and disgrace of all ancient and goodly reliques." — Extracted from a book entitled *Durham Cathedral, as it stood before the Dissolution of the Monastery.* It appears, from the old metrical history, that the above-mentioned banner was carried by the Earl of Surrey to Flodden Field.

23. It is so called to this day, and is thus described by Dr. Whitaker: — "Rylstone Fell yet exhibits a monument of the old warfare between the Nortons and Cliffords. On a point of very high ground, commanding an immense prospect, and protected by two deep ravines, are the remains of a square tower, expressly said by Dodsworth to have been built by Richard Norton. The walls are of strong grout-work, about four feet thick. It seems to have been three stories high. Breaches have been industriously made in all the sides, almost to the ground, to render it untenable.

"But Norton Tower was probably a sort of pleasure-house in summer, as there are, adjoining to it, several large mounds (two of them are pretty entire), of which no other account can be given than that they were butts for large companies of archers.

"The place is savagely wild, and admirably adapted to the uses of a watch tower."

24. "After the attainder of Richard Norton, his estates were forfeited to the crown, where they remained till the 2d or 3d of James; they were then granted to Francis Earl of Cumberland." From an accurate sur-

vey made at that time, several particulars have been extracted by Dr. W. It appears that "the mansion-house was then in decay. Immediately adjoining is a close, called the Vivery, so called, undoubtedly, from the French Vivier, or modern Latin Vivarium; for there are near the house large remains of a pleasure-ground, such as were introduced in the earlier part of Eliza-beth's time, with topiary works, fish-ponds, an island, etc. The whole township was ranged by an hundred and thirty red deer, the property of the Lord, which, together with the wood, had, after the attainder of Mr. Norton, been committed to Sir Stephen Tempest. The wood, it seems, had been abandoned to depreda-tions, before which time it appears that the neighbour-hood must have exhibited a forest-like and sylvan scene. In this survey, among the old tenants is men-tioned one Richard Kitchen, butler to Mr. Norton, who rose in rebellion with his master, and was executed at Ripon."

25. "At the extremity of the parish of Burnsal, the valley of Wharf forks off into two great branches, one of which retains the name of Wharfdale, to the source of the river; the other is usually called Littondale, but more anciently and properly, Amerdale. Dern-brook, which runs along an obscure valley from the N.W., is derived from a Teutonic word, signifying con-cealment." — DR. WHITAKER.

26. On one of the bells of Rylstone Church, which seems coeval with the building of the tower, is this

cypher, "𝕵. 𝕹." for John Norton, and the motto, "𝕲𝖔𝖉 𝖚𝖘 𝖆𝖞𝖉𝖊."

27. Which is thus described by Dr. Whitaker: "On the plain summit of the hill are the foundations of a strong wall stretching from the S. W. to the N. E. corner of the tower, and to the edge of a very deep glen. From this glen, a ditch, several hundred yards long, runs south to another deep and rugged ravine. On the N. and W., where the banks are very steep, no wall or mound is discoverable, paling being the only fence that could stand on such ground.

"From the Minstrelsy of the Scottish Border, it appears that such pounds for deer, sheep, etc., were far from being uncommon in the south of Scotland. The principle of them was something like that of a wire mouse-trap. On the declivity of a steep hill, the bottom and sides of which were fenced so as to be impassable, a wall was constructed nearly level with the surface on the outside, yet so high within, that without wings it was impossible to escape in the opposite direction. Care was probably taken that these enclosures should contain better feed than the neighbouring parks or forests; and whoever is acquainted with the habits of these sequacious animals, will easily conceive, that if the leader was once tempted to descend into the snare, a herd would follow."

I cannot conclude without recommending to the notice of all lovers of beautiful scenery Bolton Abbey and its neighbourhood. This enchanting spot belongs to the Duke of Devonshire; and the superintendence of it has for some years been entrusted to the Rev. William Carr, who has most skilfully opened out its features; and, in whatever he has added, has done justice to the place, by working with an invisible hand of Art in the very spirit of Nature.

28. In this Sonnet I am under some obligations to one of an Italian author, to which I cannot refer.

29. See Note to "The King of Sweden," p. 286.

30. See Laborde's *Character of the Spanish People;* from him the statement of these last lines is taken.

31.   Ivi vivea giocondo e i suoi pensieri
          Erano tutti rose.

The Translator had not skill to come nearer to his original.

32. In justice to the Author, I subjoin the original: —

          —— e degli amici
          Non lasciava languire i bei pensieri.

33. Sertorius.

34. A local word for Sledge.

35. A word common in the country, signifying shelter, as in Scotland.

36. Loughrigg Tarn, alluded to in the foregoing Epistle, resembles, though much smaller in compass, the Lake Nemi, or *Speculum Dianæ* as it is often called, not only in its clear waters and circular form, and the beauty immediately surrounding it, but also as being overlooked by the eminence of Langdale Pikes as Lake

Nemi is by that of Monte Calvo. Since this Epistle was written Loughrigg Tarn has lost much of its beauty by the felling of many natural clumps of wood, relics of the old forest, particularly upon the farm called "The Oaks," so called from the abundance of that tree which grew there.

It is to be regretted, upon public grounds, that Sir George Beaumont did not carry into effect his intention of constructing here a Summer Retreat in the style I have described; as his taste would have set an example how buildings, with all the accommodations modern society requires, might be introduced even into the most secluded parts of this country without injuring their native character.

37. Black Comb stands at the southern extremity of Cumberland: its base covers a much greater extent of ground than any other mountain in those parts; and, from its situation, the summit commands a more extensive view than any other point in Britain.

38. For the account of these long-lived trees, see Pliny's *Natural History*, lib. xvi, cap. 44; and for the features in the character of Protesilaus see the "Iphigenia in Aulis" of Euripides. Virgil places the Shade of Laodamia in a mournful region, among unhappy Lovers.

> "—— His Laodamia,
>   It comes. ——"

39. This poem began with the following stanza, which has been displaced on account of its detaining the reader too long from the subject, and as rather

precluding, than preparing for, the due effect of the
allusion to the genius of Plato: —

> "Fair is the Swan, whose majesty, prevailing
> O'er breezeless water, on Locarno's lake,
> Bears him on while proudly sailing
> He leaves behind a moon-illumined wake:
> Behold! the mantling spirit of reserve
> Fashions his neck into a goodly curve;
> An arch thrown back between luxuriant wings
> Of whitest garniture, like fir-tree boughs
> To which, on some unruffled morning, clings
> A flaky weight of winter's purest snows!
> — Behold! — as with a gushing impulse heaves
> That downy prow, and softly cleaves
> The mirror of the crystal flood,
> Vanish inverted hill, and shadowy wood,
> And pendent rocks, where'er, in gliding state,
> Winds the mute Creature without visible Mate
> Or Rival, save the Queen of night
> Showering down a silver light,
> From heaven, upon her chosen Favourite!"

40. On the banks of the River Nid, near Knares-
borough.

41. See the Vision of Mirza in the *Spectator*.

VOLUME VI

THE EXCURSION

1. At the risk of giving a shock to the prejudices of artificial society, I have ever been ready to pay homage to the aristocracy of Nature; under a conviction that vigorous human-heartedness is the constituent principle of true taste. It may still, however, be satisfactory to have prose testimony how far a Character, employed for purposes of imagination, is founded upon general fact. I, therefore, subjoin an extract from an author who had opportunities of being well acquainted with a class of men, from whom my own personal knowledge emboldened me to draw this portrait.

"We learn from Cæsar and other Roman Writers, that the travelling merchants who frequented Gaul and other barbarous countries, either newly conquered by the Roman arms, or bordering on the Roman conquests, were ever the first to make the inhabitants of those countries familiarly acquainted with the Roman modes of life, and to inspire them with an inclination to follow the Roman fashions, and to enjoy Roman conveniences. In North America, travelling merchants from the Settlements have done and continue to do much more towards civilising the Indian natives, than all the missionaries, papist or protestant, who have ever been sent among them.

"It is farther to be observed, for the credit of this

most useful class of men, that they commonly contribute, by their personal manners, no less than by the sale of their wares, to the refinement of the people among whom they travel. Their dealings form them to great quickness of wit and acuteness of judgment. Having constant occasion to recommend themselves and their goods, they acquire habits of the most obliging attention, and the most insinuating address. As in their peregrinations they have opportunity of contemplating the manners of various men and various cities, they become eminently skilled in the knowledge of the world. *As they wander, each alone, through thinly-inhabited districts, they form habits of reflection and of sublime contemplation.* With all these qualifications, no wonder that they should often be, in remote parts of the country, the best mirrors of fashion, and censors of manners; and should contribute much to polish the roughness and soften the rusticity of our peasantry. It is not more than twenty or thirty years since a young man going from any part of Scotland to England, of purpose to *carry the pack*, was considered as going to lead the life and acquire the fortune of a gentleman. When, after twenty years' absence in that honourable line of employment, he returned with his acquisitions to his native country, he was regarded as a gentleman to all intents and purposes." —HERON's *Journey in Scotland*, vol. i, p. 89.

2. *Lost in unsearchable eternity!* Since this paragraph was composed, I have read with so much pleasure, in

Burnet's Theory of the Earth, a passage expressing corresponding sentiments, excited by objects of a similar nature, that I cannot forbear to transcribe it.

"Siquod verò Natura nobis dedit spectaculum, in hâc tellure, verè gratum, et philosopho dignum, id semel mihi contigisse arbitror; cùm ex celsissimâ rupe speculabundus ad oram maris Mediterranei, hinc æquor cæruleum, illinc tractus Alpinos prospexi; nihil quidem magìs dispar aut dissimile, nec in suo genere, magìs egregium et singulare. Hoc theatrum ego facilè prætulerim Romanis cunctis, Græcisve; atque id quod natura hîc spectandum exhibet, scenicis ludis omnibus, aut amphitheatri certaminibus. Nihil hîc elegans aut venustum, sed ingens et magnificum, et quod placet magnitudine suâ et quâdam specie immensitatis. Hinc intuebar maris æquabilem superficiem, usque et usque diffusam, quantum maximùm oculorum acies ferri potuit; illinc disruptissimam terræ faciem, et vastas moles variè elevatas aut depressas, erectas, propendentes, reclinatas, coacervatas, omni situ inæquali et turbido. Placuit, ex hâc parte, Naturæ unitas et simplicitas, et inexhausta quædam planities; ex alterâ, multiformis confusio magnorum corporum et insanæ rerum strages: quas cùm intuebar, non urbis alicujus aut oppidi, sed confracti mundi rudera, ante oculos habere mihi visus sum.

"In singulis ferè montibus erat aliquid insolens et mirabile, sed præ cæteris mihi placebat illa, quâ sedebam, rupes; erat maxima et altissima, et quâ terram respiciebat, molliori ascensu altitudinem suam dissimulabat: quà verò mare, horrendùm præceps, et quasi ad perpendiculum facta, instar parietis. Prætereà facies illa marina adeò erat lævis ac uniformis (quod in rupibus aliquando observare licet) ac si scissa fuisset à summo ad imum, in illo plano; vel terræ motu aliquo, aut fulmine, divulsa.

"Ima pars rupis erat cava, recessusque habuit, et saxeos specus, euntes in vacuum montem; sive naturâ pridem factos, sive exesos mari, et undarum crebris ictibus: In hos enim cum impetu ruebant et fragore, æstuantis maris fluctus; quos iterum spumantes reddidit antrum, et quasi ab imo ventre evomuit.

"Dextrum latus montis erat præruptum, aspero saxo et nudâ caute: sinistrum non adeò neglexerat Natura, arboribus utpote ornatum: et prope pedem montis rivus limpidæ aquæ prorupit; qui cùm vicinam vallem irrigaverat, lento motu serpens, et per varios mæandros, quasi ad protrahendam vitam, in magno mari absorptus subito periit. Denique in summo vertice promontorii, commodè eminebat saxum, cui insidebam contemplabundus. Vale augusta sedes. Rege digna: Augusta rupes, semper mihi memoranda!" P. 89. *Telluris Theoria sacra, etc., Editio secunda.*

3. *Of Mississippi, or that northern stream.* "A man is supposed to improve by going out into the *World*, by visiting *London*. Artificial man does; he extends with his sphere; but, alas! that sphere is microscopic; it is formed of minutiæ, and he surrenders his genuine vision to the artist, in order to embrace it in his ken. His

bodily senses grow acute, even to barren and inhuman pruriency; while his mental become proportionately obtuse. The reverse is the Man of Mind: he who is placed in the sphere of Nature and of God, might be a mock at Tattersall's and Brooks's, and a sneer at St. James's: he would certainly be swallowed alive by the first *Pizarro* that crossed him: — But when he walks along the river of Amazons; when he rests his eye on the unrivalled Andes; when he measures the long and watered savannah; or contemplates, from a sudden promontory, the distant, vast Pacific — and feels himself a freeman in this vast theatre, and commanding each ready produced fruit of this wilderness, and each progeny of this stream — his exultation is not less than imperial. He is as gentle, too, as he is great: his emotions of tenderness keep pace with his elevation of sentiment; for he says, 'These were made by a good Being, who, unsought by me, placed me here to enjoy them.' He becomes at once a child and a king. His mind is in himself; from hence he argues, and from hence he acts, and he argues unerringly, and acts magisterially: his mind in himself is also in his God; and therefore he loves, and therefore he soars." — From the notes upon "The Hurricane," a Poem, by William Gilbert.

The Reader, I am sure, will thank me for the above quotation, which, though from a strange book, is one of the finest passages of modern English prose.

4. *'T is, by comparison,* etc. See, upon this subject, Baxter's most interesting review of his own opinions

and sentiments in the decline of life. It may be found (lately reprinted) in Dr. Wordsworth's *Ecclesiastical Biography.*

5. This subject is treated at length in the Ode — "Intimations of Immortality."

6. The passage quoted from Daniel is taken from a poem addressed to the Lady Margaret, Countess of Cumberland, and the two last lines, printed in Italics, are by him translated from Seneca. The whole Poem is very beautiful. I will transcribe four stanzas from it, as they contain an admirable picture of the state of a wise Man's mind in a time of public commotion.

> "Nor is he moved with all the thunder-cracks
> Of tyrant's threats, or with the surly brow
> Of Power, that proudly sits on others' crimes;
> Charged with more crying sins than those he checks
> The storms of sad confusion that may grow
> Up in the present for the coming times,
> Appal not him; that hath no side at all,
> But of himself, and knows the worst can fall.

> "Although his heart (so near allied to earth)
> Cannot but pity the perplexèd state
> Of troublous and distressed mortality,
> That thus make way unto the ugly birth
> Of their own sorrows, and do still beget
> Affliction upon imbecility:
> Yet seeing thus the course of things must run,
> He looks thereon not strange, but as fore-done.

> "And whilst distraught ambition compasses,
> And is encompassed, while as craft deceives,
> And is deceived: whilst man doth ransack man,

[182]

And builds on blood, and rises by distress;
And th' Inheritance of desolation leaves
To great-expecting hopes: He looks thereon,
As from the shore of peace, with unwet eye,
And bears no venture in Impiety.

"Thus, Lady, fares that man that hath prepared
A rest for his desires; and sees all things
Beneath him; and hath learned this book of man,
Full of the notes of frailty; and compared
The best of glory with her sufferings:
By whom, I see, you labour all you can
To plant your heart! and set your thoughts as near
His glorious mansion as your powers can bear."

7.   *Leo.* You, Sir, could help me to the history
Of half these graves?
       Priest.   For eight-score winters past,
With what I've witnessed, and with what I've heard,
Perhaps I might; . . .
By turning o'er these hillocks one by one,
We two could travel, Sir, through a strange round;
Yet all in the broad highway of the world.
                                        The Brothers.

8. "And suffering Nature grieved that one should die."
                          Southey's *Retrospect.*

9. The sentiments and opinions here uttered are in
unison with those expressed in the following Essay
upon Epitaphs, which was furnished by me for Mr.
Coleridge's periodical work, *The Friend;* and as they
are dictated by a spirit congenial to that which pervades this and the two succeeding books, the sympathising reader will not be displeased to see the Essay
here annexed.

[183]

ESSAY UPON EPITAPHS

It needs scarcely be said, that an Epitaph presupposes a Monument, upon which it is to be engraven. Almost all Nations have wished that certain external signs should point out the places where their dead are interred. Among savage tribes unacquainted with letters this has mostly been done either by rude stones placed near the graves, or by mounds of earth raised over them. This custom proceeded obviously from a twofold desire: first to guard the remains of the deceased from irreverent approach or from savage violation: and secondly to preserve their memory. "Never any," says Camden, "neglected burial but some savage nations; as the Bactrians, which cast their dead to the dogs; some varlet philosophers, as Diogenes, who desired to be devoured of fishes; some dissolute courtiers, as Mæcenas, who was wont to say, Non tumulum curo; sepelit natura relictos.

'I'm careless of a grave: — Nature her dead will save.'"

As soon as nations had learned the use of letters, epitaphs were inscribed upon these monuments; in order that their intention might be more surely and adequately fulfilled. I have derived monuments and epitaphs from two sources of feeling, but these do in fact resolve themselves into one. The invention of epitaphs, Weever, in his *Discourse of Funeral Monuments*, says rightly, "proceeded from the presage or fore-feeling of immortality, implanted in all men naturally, and is

[184]

referred to the scholars of Linus the Theban poet, who
flourished about the year of the world two thousand
seven hundred; who first bewailed this Linus their Master, when he was slain, in doleful verses, then called of
him Œlina, afterwards Epitaphia, for that they were first
sung at burials, after engraved upon the sepulchres."

And, verily, without the consciousness of a principle
of immortality in the human soul, Man could never
have had awakened in him the desire to live in the remembrance of his fellows: mere love, or the yearning
of kind towards kind, could not have produced it. The
dog or horse perishes in the field, or in the stall, by the
side of his companions, and is incapable of anticipating
the sorrow with which his surrounding associates shall
bemoan his death, or pine for his loss; he cannot pre-
conceive this regret, he can form no thought of it; and
therefore cannot possibly have a desire to leave such
regret or remembrance behind him. Add to the principle of love which exists in the inferior animals, the
faculty of reason which exists in Man alone; will the
conjunction of these account for the desire? Doubtless it
is a necessary consequence of this conjunction; yet not,
I think, as a direct result, but only to be come at through
an intermediate thought, viz. that of an intimation or
assurance within us, that some part of our nature is
imperishable. At least the precedence, in order of
birth, of one feeling to the other, is unquestionable.
If we look back upon the days of childhood, we shall
find that the time is not in remembrance when, with

respect to our own individual Being, the mind was without this assurance; whereas, the wish to be remembered by our friends or kindred after death, or even in absence, is, as we shall discover, a sensation that does not form itself till the *social* feelings have been developed, and the Reason has connected itself with a wide range of objects. Forlorn, and cut off from communication with the best part of his nature, must that man be, who should derive the sense of immortality, as it exists in the mind of a child, from the same unthinking gaiety or liveliness of animal spirits with which the lamb in the meadow or any other irrational creature is endowed; who should ascribe it, in short, to blank ignorance in the child; to an inability arising from the imperfect state of his faculties to come, in any point of his being, into contact with a notion of death; or to an unreflecting acquiescence in what has been instilled into him! Has such an unfolder of the mysteries of nature, though he may have forgotten his former self, ever noticed the early, obstinate, and unappeasable inquisitiveness of children upon the subject of origination? This single fact proves outwardly the monstrousness of those suppositions: for, if we had no direct external testimony that the minds of very young children meditate feelingly upon death and immortality, these inquiries, which we all know they are perpetually making concerning the *whence*, do necessarily include correspondent habits of interrogation concerning the *whither*. Origin and tendency are notions inseparably co-relative. Never did a child stand by the side of a running stream, pondering within himself what power was the feeder of the perpetual current, from what never-wearied sources the body of water was supplied, but he must have been inevitably propelled to follow this question by another: "Towards what abyss is it in progress? what receptacle can contain the mighty influx?" And the spirit of the answer must have been, though the word might be sea or ocean, accompanied perhaps with an image gathered from a map, or from the real object in nature, — these might have been the *letter*, but the *spirit* of the answer must have been *as* inevitably, — a receptacle without bounds or dimensions; — nothing less than infinity. We may, then, be justified in asserting, that the sense of immortality, if not a co-existent and twin birth with Reason, is among the earliest of her offspring: and we may further assert, that from these conjoined, and under their countenance, the human affections are gradually formed and opened out. This is not the place to enter into the recesses of these investigations; but the subject requires me here to make a plain avowal, that, for my own part, it is to me inconceivable, that the sympathies of love towards each other, which grow with our growth, could ever attain any new strength, or even preserve the old, after we had received from the outward senses the impression of death, and were in the habit of having that impression daily renewed and its accompanying feeling brought home to ourselves, and to those we love; if the same were not counteracted by those communications with our internal Being, which are anterior to all these experiences, and with which revelation coincides, and has through that coincidence alone (for otherwise it could not possess it) a power to affect us. I confess, with me the conviction is absolute that, if the impression and sense of death were not thus counterbalanced, such a hollowness would pervade the whole system of things, such a want of correspondence and consistency, a disproportion so astounding betwixt means and ends, that there could be no repose, no joy. Were we to grow up unfostered by this genial warmth, a frost would chill the spirit, so penetrating and powerful that there could be no motions of the life of love; and infinitely less could we have any wish to be remembered after we had passed away from a world in which each man had moved about like a shadow. — If, then, in a creature endowed with the faculties of foresight and reason, the social affections could not have unfolded themselves uncountenanced by the faith that Man is an immortal being, and if, consequently, neither could the individual dying have had a desire to survive in the remembrance of his fellows, nor on their side could they have felt a wish to preserve for future times vestiges of the departed; it follows, as a final inference, that without the belief in immortality, wherein these several desires originate, neither monuments nor epitaphs, in affectionate or laudatory commemoration of the deceased, could have existed in the world.

Simonides, it is related, upon landing in a strange
country, found the corse of an unknown person lying
by the seaside; he buried it, and was honoured throughout Greece for the piety of that act. Another ancient
Philosopher, chancing to fix his eyes upon a dead
body, regarded the same with slight, if not with contempt, saying, "See the shell of the flown bird!" But
it is not to be supposed that the moral and tender-
hearted Simonides was incapable of the lofty movements of thought to which that other Sage gave way
at the moment while his soul was intent only upon the
indestructible being; nor, on the other hand, that he,
in whose sight a lifeless human body was of no more
value than the worthless shell from which the living
fowl had departed, would not, in a different mood of
mind, have been affected by those earthly considerations
which had incited the philosophic Poet to the performance of that pious duty. And with regard to this latter
we may be assured that, if he had been destitute of
the capability of communing with the more exalted
thoughts that appertain to human nature, he would
have cared no more for the corse of the stranger than
for the dead body of a seal or porpoise which might have
been cast up by the waves. We respect the corporeal
frame of Man, not merely because it is the habitation
of a rational, but of an immortal Soul. Each of these
Sages was in sympathy with the best feelings of our
nature; feelings which, though they seem opposite to
each other, have another and a finer connection than

[189]

that of contrast. — It is a connection formed through the subtle progress by which, both in the natural and the moral world, qualities pass insensibly into their contraries, and things revolve upon each other. As, in sailing upon the orb of this planet, a voyage towards the regions where the sun sets conducts gradually to the quarter where we have been accustomed to behold it come forth at its rising; and, in like manner, a voyage towards the east, the birth-place in our imagination of the morning, leads finally to the quarter where the sun is last seen when he departs from our eyes; so the contemplative Soul, travelling in the direction of mortality, advances to the country of everlasting life; and, in like manner, may she continue to explore those cheerful tracts till she is brought back, for her advantage and benefit, to the land of transitory things — of sorrow and of tears.

On a midway point, therefore, which commands the thoughts and feelings of the two Sages whom we have represented in contrast, does the Author of that species of composition, the laws of which it is our present purpose to explain, take his stand. Accordingly, recurring to the twofold desire of guarding the remains of the deceased and preserving their memory, it may be said that a sepulchral monument is a tribute to a man as a human being; and that an epitaph (in the ordinary meaning attached to the word) includes this general feeling and something more; and is a record to preserve the memory of the dead, as a tribute due to his individual worth, for a satisfaction to the sorrowing

hearts of the survivors, and for the common benefit of
the living: which record is to be accomplished, not in
a general manner, but where it can, in *close connection
with the bodily remains of the deceased:* and these, it may
be added, among the modern nations of Europe, are
deposited within, or contiguous to, their places of worship. In ancient times, as is well known, it was the custom to bury the dead beyond the walls of towns and
cities; and among the Greeks and Romans they were
frequently interred by the waysides.

I could here pause with pleasure, and invite the
Reader to indulge with me in contemplation of the advantages which must have attended such a practice.
We might ruminate upon the beauty which the monuments, thus placed, must have borrowed from the
surrounding images of Nature — from the trees, the
wild flowers, from a stream running perhaps within
sight or hearing, from the beaten road stretching its
weary length hard by. Many tender similitudes must
these objects have presented to the mind of the traveller leaning upon one of the tombs, or reposing in the
coolness of its shade, whether he had halted from
weariness or in compliance with the invitation, "Pause,
Traveller!" so often found upon the monuments. And
to its epitaph also must have been supplied strong appeals to visible appearances or immediate impressions,
lively and affecting analogies of life as a journey —
death as a sleep overcoming the tired wayfarer — of
misfortune as a storm that falls suddenly upon him —

[191]

of beauty as a flower that passeth away, or of innocent pleasure as one that may be gathered — of virtue that standeth firm as a rock against the beating waves — of hope "undermined insensibly like the poplar by the side of the river that has fed it," or blasted in a moment like a pine-tree by the stroke of lightning upon the mountain-top — of admonitions and heart-stirring remembrances, like a refreshing breeze that comes without warning, or the taste of the waters of an unexpected fountain. These and similar suggestions must have given, formerly, to the language of the senseless stone a voice enforced and endeared by the benignity of that nature with which it was in unison. — We, in modern times, have lost much of these advantages; and they are but in a small degree counterbalanced to the inhabitants of large towns and cities by the custom of depositing the dead within, or contiguous to, their places of worship; however splendid or imposing may be the appearance of those edifices, or however interesting or salutary the recollections associated with them. Even were it not true that tombs lose their monitory virtue when thus obtruded upon the notice of men occupied with the cares of the world, and too often sullied and defiled by those cares, yet still, when death is in our thoughts, nothing can make amends for the want of the soothing influences of Nature, and for the absence of those types of renovation and decay which the fields and woods offer to the notice of the serious and contemplative mind. To feel the force of this sentiment, let a man only compare in imagination the unsightly manner in which our monuments are crowded together in the busy, noisy, unclean, and almost grassless churchyard of a large town, with the still seclusion of a Turkish cemetery, in some remote place, and yet further sanctified by the grove of cypress in which it is embosomed. Thoughts in the same temper as these have already been expressed with true sensibility by an ingenuous Poet of the present day. The subject of his poem is "All Saints Church, Derby": he has been deploring the forbidding and unseemly appearance of its burial-ground, and uttering a wish that in past times the practice had been adopted of interring the inhabitants of large towns in the country: —

> "Then in some rural, calm, sequestered spot
>   Where healing Nature her benignant look
>   Ne'er changes, save at that lorn season, when,
> With tresses drooping o'er her sable stole,
>   She yearly mourns the mortal doom of man,
>   Her noblest work, (so Israel's virgins erst,
> With annual moan upon the mountains wept
> Their fairest gone,) there in that rural scene,
> So placid, so congenial to the wish
> The Christian feels, of peaceful rest within
> The silent grave, I would have stayed:
>
>   .   .   .   .
>
> — wandered forth, where the cold dew of heaven
> Lay on the humbler graves around, what time
> The pale moon gazed upon the turfy mounds,
> Pensive, as though like me, in lonely muse,
> 'T were brooding on the dead inhumed beneath.

[193]

There while with him, the holy man of Uz,
O'er human destiny I sympathised,
Counting the long, long periods prophecy
Decrees to roll, ere the great day arrives
Of resurrection, oft the blue-eyed Spring
Had met me with her blossoms, as the Dove,
Of old, returned with olive leaf, to cheer
The Patriarch mourning o'er a world destroyed:
And I would bless her visit; for to me
'T is sweet to trace the consonance that links
As one, the works of Nature and the word
Of God. ——"   JOHN EDWARDS.

A village churchyard, lying as it does in the lap of
Nature, may indeed be most favourably contrasted
with that of a town of crowded population; and se-
pulture therein combines many of the best tendencies
which belong to the mode practised by the Ancients
with others peculiar to itself. The sensations of pious
cheerfulness, which attend the celebration of the sab-
bath-day in rural places, are profitably chastised by
the sight of the graves of kindred and friends, gathered
together in that general home towards which the
thoughtful yet happy spectators themselves are jour-
neying. Hence a parish church, in the stillness of the
country, is a visible centre of a community of the living
and the dead; a point to which are habitually referred
the nearest concerns of both.

As, then, both in cities and in villages, the dead are
deposited in close connection with our places of worship, with us the composition of an epitaph naturally
turns, still more than among the nations of antiquity,

upon the most serious and solemn affections of the
human mind; upon departed worth — upon personal or
social sorrow and admiration — upon religion, individual and social — upon time, and upon eternity. Accordingly, it suffices, in ordinary cases, to secure a composition of this kind from censure, that it contain
nothing that shall shock or be inconsistent with this
spirit. But, to entitle an epitaph to praise, more than
this is necessary. It ought to contain some thought
or feeling belonging to the mortal or immortal part of
our nature touchingly expressed; and if that be done,
however general or even trite the sentiment may be,
every man of pure mind will read the words with pleasure
and gratitude. A husband bewails a wife; a parent
breathes a sigh of disappointed hope over a lost child;
a son utters a sentiment of filial reverence for a departed father or mother; a friend perhaps inscribes an
encomium recording the companionable qualities, or
the solid virtues, of the tenant of the grave, whose departure has left a sadness upon his memory. This and
a pious admonition to the living, and a humble expression of Christian confidence in immortality, is the language of a thousand churchyards; and it does not often
happen that anything, in a greater degree discriminate
or appropriate to the dead or to the living, is to be found
in them. This want of discrimination has been ascribed
by Dr. Johnson, in his Essay upon the epitaphs of Pope,
to two causes: first, the scantiness of the objects of
human praise; and, secondly, the want of variety in

the characters of men; or, to use his own words, "to the fact, that the greater part of mankind have no character at all." Such language may be holden without blame among the generalities of common conversation; but does not become a critic and a moralist speaking seriously upon a serious subject. The objects of admiration in human nature are not scanty, but abundant, and every man has a character of his own to the eye that has skill to perceive it. The real cause of the acknowledged want of discrimination in sepulchral memorials is this: That to analyse the characters of others, especially of those whom we love, is not a common or natural employment of men at any time. We are not anxious unerringly to understand the constitution of the minds of those who have soothed, who have cheered, who have supported us; with whom we have been long and daily pleased or delighted. The affections are their own justification. The light of love in our hearts is a satisfactory evidence that there is a body of worth in the minds of our friends or kindred, whence that light has proceeded. We shrink from the thought of placing their merits and defects to be weighed against each other in the nice balance of pure intellect; nor do we find much temptation to detect the shades by which a good quality of virtue is discriminated in them from an excellence known by the same general name as it exists in the mind of another; and least of all do we incline to these refinements when under the pressure of sorrow, admiration, or regret, or when actuated by any of those feelings which incite men to prolong the memory of their friends and kindred by records placed in the bosom of the all-uniting and equalising receptacle of the dead.

The first requisite, then, in an Epitaph is, that it should speak, in a tone which shall sink into the heart, the general language of humanity as connected with the subject of death — the source from which an epitaph proceeds — of death, and of life. To be born and to die are the two points in which all men feel themselves to be in absolute coincidence. This general language may be uttered so strikingly as to entitle an epitaph to high praise; yet it cannot lay claim to the highest unless other excellences be superadded. Passing through all intermediate steps, we will attempt to determine at once what these excellences are, and wherein consists the perfection of this species of composition. — It will be found to lie in a due proportion of the common or universal feeling of humanity to sensations excited by a distinct and clear conception, conveyed to the reader's mind, of the individual whose death is deplored and whose memory is to be preserved; at least of his character as, after death, it appeared to those who loved him and lament his loss. The general sympathy ought to be quickened, provoked, and diversified, by particular thoughts, actions, images, — circumstances of age, occupation, manner of life, prosperity which the deceased had known, or adversity to which he had been subject; and these ought to be bound together and solemnised into one harmony by the general sympathy.

The two powers should temper, restrain, and exalt each other. The reader ought to know who and what the man was whom he is called upon to think of with interest. A distinct conception should be given (implicitly where it can, rather than explicitly) of the individual lamented. — But the writer of an epitaph is not an anatomist, who dissects the internal frame of the mind; he is not even a painter, who executes a portrait at leisure and in entire tranquillity: his delineation, we must remember, is performed by the side of the grave; and, what is more, the grave of one whom he loves and admires. What purity and brightness is that virtue clothed in, the image of which must no longer bless our living eyes! The character of a deceased friend or beloved kinsman is not seen — no, nor ought to be seen — otherwise than as a tree through a tender haze or a luminous mist, that spiritualises and beautifies it; that takes away, indeed, but only to the end that the parts which are not abstracted may appear more dignified and lovely; may impress and affect the more. Shall we say, then, that this is not truth, not a faithful image; and that, accordingly, the purposes of commemoration cannot be answered? — It *is* truth, and of the highest order; for, though doubtless things are not apparent which did exist; yet, the object being looked at through this medium, parts and proportions are brought into distinct view which before had been only imperfectly or unconsciously seen: it is truth hallowed by love — the joint offspring of the worth of the dead

and the affections of the living! This may easily be
brought to the test. Let one, whose eyes have been
sharpened by personal hostility to discover what was
amiss in the character of a good man, hear the tidings
of his death, and what a change is wrought in a moment!
Enmity melts away; and, as it disappears, unsightli-
ness, disproportion, and deformity, vanish; and, through
the influence of commiseration, a harmony of love and
beauty succeeds. Bring such a man to the tombstone
on which shall be inscribed an epitaph on his adversary,
composed in the spirit which we have recommended.
Would he turn from it as from an idle tale? No; — the
thoughtful look, the sigh, and perhaps the involuntary
tear, would testify that it had a sane, a generous, and
good meaning; and that on the writer's mind had remained an impression which was a true abstract of the
character of the deceased; that his gifts and graces
were remembered in the simplicity in which they ought
to be remembered. The composition and quality of
the mind of a virtuous man, contemplated by the side
of the grave where his body is mouldering, ought to
appear, and be felt as something midway between what
he was on earth walking about with his living frailties,
and what he may be presumed to be as a Spirit in
Heaven.

It suffices, therefore, that the trunk and the main
branches of the worth of the deceased be boldly and
unaffectedly represented. Any further detail, minutely
and scrupulously pursued, especially if this be done

with laborious and antithetic discriminations, must inevitably frustrate its own purpose; forcing the passing Spectator to this conclusion, — either that the dead did not possess the merits ascribed to him, or that they who have raised a monument to his memory, and must therefore be supposed to have been closely connected with him, were incapable of perceiving those merits; or at least during the act of composition had lost sight of them; for, the understanding having been so busy in its petty occupation, how could the heart of the mourner be other than cold? and in either of these cases, whether the fault be on the part of the buried person or the survivors, the memorial is unaffecting and profitless.

Much better is it to fall short in discrimination than to pursue it too far, or to labour it unfeelingly. For in no place are we so much disposed to dwell upon those points of nature and condition wherein all men resemble each other, as in the temple where the universal Father is worshipped, or by the side of the grave which gathers all human Beings to itself, and "equalises the lofty and the low." We suffer and we weep with the same heart; we love and are anxious for one another in one spirit; our hopes look to the same quarter; and the virtues by which we are all to be furthered and supported, as patience, meekness, goodwill, justice, temperance, and temperate desires, are in an equal degree the concern of us all. Let an Epitaph, then, contain at least these acknowledgments to our common nature; nor let the sense of their importance be sacrificed to

a balance of opposite qualities or minute distinctions
in individual character; which if they do not (as will
for the most part be the case), when examined, resolve
themselves into a trick of words, will, even when they
are true and just, for the most part be grievously out
of place; for, as it is probable that few only have
explored these intricacies of human nature, so can the
tracing of them be interesting only to a few. But an
epitaph is not a proud writing shut up for the studious:
it is exposed to all — to the wise and the most ignorant;
it is condescending, perspicuous, and lovingly solicits
regard; its story and admonitions are brief, that the
thoughtless, the busy, and indolent, may not be de-
terred, nor the impatient tired: the stooping old man
cons the engraven record like a second horn-book; —
the child is proud that he can read it; — and the stranger
is introduced through its mediation to the company of
a friend: it is concerning all, and for all: — in the churchyard it is open to the day; the sun looks down upon the
stone, and the rains of heaven beat against it.

Yet, though the writer who would excite sympathy
is bound in this case, more than in any other, to give
proof that he himself has been moved, it is to be remembered that to raise a monument is a sober and a
reflective act; that the inscription which it bears is
intended to be permanent and for universal perusal;
and that, for this reason, the thoughts and feelings expressed should be permanent also — liberated from that
weakness and anguish of sorrow which is in nature

[201]

transitory, and which with instinctive decency retires
from notice. The passions should be subdued, the emotions controlled; strong, indeed, but nothing ungovern-
able or wholly involuntary. Seemliness requires this,
and truth requires it also: for how can the narrator
otherwise be trusted? Moreover, a grave is a tran-
quillising object: resignation in course of time springs
up from it as naturally as the wild flowers, besprinkling
the turf with which it may be covered, or gathering
round the monument by which it is defended. The very
form and substance of the monument which has received the inscription, and the appearance of the letters,
testifying with what a slow and laborious hand they
must have been engraven, might seem to reproach the
author who had given way upon this occasion to trans-
ports of mind, or to quick turns of conflicting passions;
though the same might constitute the life and beauty
of a funeral oration or elegiac poem.

These sensations and judgments, acted upon perhaps
unconsciously, have been one of the main causes why
epitaphs so often personate the deceased, and represent
him as speaking from his own tomb-stone. The departed Mortal is introduced telling you himself that his
pains are gone; that a state of rest is come; and he con-
jures you to weep for him no longer. He admonishes
with the voice of one experienced in the vanity of those
affections which are confined to earthly objects, and
gives a verdict like a superior Being, performing the
office of a judge, who has no temptations to mislead

him, and whose decision cannot but be dispassionate. Thus is death disarmed of its sting, and affliction unsubstantialised. By this tender fiction, the survivors bind themselves to a sedater sorrow, and employ the intervention of the imagination in order that the reason may speak her own language earlier than she would otherwise have been enabled to do. This shadowy interposition also harmoniously unites the two worlds of the living and the dead by their appropriate affections. And it may be observed that here we have an additional proof of the propriety with which sepulchral inscriptions were referred to the consciousness of immortality as their primal source.

I do not speak with a wish to recommend that an epitaph should be cast in this mould preferably to the still more common one, in which what is said comes from the survivors directly; but rather to point out how natural those feelings are which have induced men, in all states and ranks of society, so frequently to adopt this mode. And this I have done chiefly in order that the laws which ought to govern the composition of the other may be better understood. This latter mode, namely, that in which the survivors speak in their own persons, seems to me upon the whole greatly preferable, as it admits a wider range of notices; and, above all, because, excluding the fiction which is the groundwork of the other, it rests upon a more solid basis.

Enough has been said to convey our notion of a perfect epitaph; but it must be borne in mind that one is meant which will best answer the *general* ends of that species of composition. According to the course pointed out, the worth of private life, through all varieties of situation and character, will be most honourably and profitably preserved in memory. Nor would the model recommended less suit public men in all instances, save of those persons who by the greatness of their services in the employments of peace or war, or by the surpassing excellence of their works in art, literature, or science, have made themselves not only universally known, but have filled the heart of their country with everlasting gratitude. Yet I must here pause to correct myself. In describing the general tenor of thought which epitaphs ought to hold, I have omitted to say, that if it be the *actions* of a man, or even some *one* conspicuous or beneficial act of local or general utility, which have distinguished him, and excited a desire that he should be remembered, then, of course, ought the attention to be directed chiefly to those actions or that act: and such sentiments dwelt upon as naturally arise out of them or it. Having made this necessary distinction, I proceed. — The mighty benefactors of mankind, as they are not only known by the immediate survivors, but will continue to be known familiarly to latest posterity, do not stand in need of biographic sketches in such a place; nor of delineations of character to individualise them. This is already done by their Works, in the memories of men. Their naked names, and a grand comprehensive sentiment of civic gratitude, patriotic love, or human admiration — or the utterance of some elementary principle most essential in the constitution of true virtue — or a declaration touching that pious humility and self-abasement, which are ever most profound as minds are most susceptible of genuine exaltation — or an intuition, communicated in adequate words, of the sublimity of intellectual power; — these are the only tribute which can here be paid — the only offering that upon such an altar would not be unworthy.

> "What needs my Shakespeare for his honoured bones
> The labour of an age in pilèd stones,
> Or that his hallowed reliques should be hid
> Under a star-ypointing pyramid?
> Dear Son of Memory, great Heir of Fame,
> What need'st thou such weak witness of thy name?
> Thou in our wonder and astonishment
> Hast built thyself a livelong monument,
> And so sepulchred, in such pomp dost lie,
> That kings for such a tomb would wish to die."

10. An instinctive taste teaches men to build their churches in flat countries with spire-steeples, which, as they cannot be referred to any other object, point as with silent finger to the sky and stars, and sometimes, when they reflect the brazen light of a rich though rainy sunset, appear like a pyramid of flame burning heavenward. See *The Friend*, by S. T. Coleridge, No. 14, p. 223.

11.   "This Sycamore oft musical with Bees;
       Such Tents the Patriarchs loved."

S. T. COLERIDGE.

12. The "Transit gloria mundi" is finely expressed in the Introduction to the Foundation-charters of some of the ancient Abbeys. Some expressions here used are taken from that of the Abbey of St. Mary's, Furness, the translation of which is as follows: —

"Considering every day the uncertainty of life, that the roses and flowers of Kings, Emperors, and Dukes, and the crowns and palms of all the great wither and decay; and that all things, with an uninterrupted course, tend to dissolution and death: I, therefore," etc.

13. Truly described from what I myself saw during my boyhood and early youth. (Fenwick note.)

14. In treating this subject, it was impossible not to recollect with gratitude the pleasing picture which in his poem of the Fleece the excellent and amiable Dyer has given of the influences of manufacturing industry upon the face of this Island. He wrote at a time when machinery was first beginning to be introduced, and his benevolent heart prompted him to augur from it nothing but good. Truth has compelled me to dwell upon the baneful effects arising out of an ill-regulated and excessive application of powers so admirable in themselves.

15. The discovery of Dr. Bell affords marvellous facilities for carrying this into effect; and it is impossible to overrate the benefit which might accrue to humanity from the universal application of this simple engine under an enlightened and conscientious government.

VOLUME VII

1. Wholly unworthy of touching upon the momentous subject here treated would that Poet be, before
whose eyes the present distresses under which this
kingdom labours could interpose a veil sufficiently thick
to hide, or even to obscure, the splendour of this great
moral triumph. If I have given way to exultation,
unchecked by these distresses, it might be sufficient
to protect me from a charge of insensibility, should I
state my own belief that the sufferings will be transitory.
Upon the wisdom of a very large majority of the British
nation rested that generosity which poured out the
treasures of this country for the deliverance of Europe:
and in the same national wisdom, presiding in time of
peace over an energy not inferior to that which has been
displayed in war, *they* confide, who encourage a firm
hope that the cup of our wealth will be gradually re-
plenished. There will, doubtless, be no few ready to indulge in regrets and repinings; and to feed a morbid
satisfaction, by aggravating these burthens in imagination; in order that calamity so confidently pro-
phesied, as it has not taken the shape which their
sagacity allotted to it, may appear as grievous as possible under another. But the body of the nation will
not quarrel with the gain, because it might have been
purchased at a less price; and, acknowledging in these
sufferings, which they feel to have been in a great
degree unavoidable, a consecration of their noble ef-

forts, they will vigorously apply themselves to remedy the evil.

Nor is it at the expense of rational patriotism, or in disregard of sound philosophy, that I have given vent to feelings tending to encourage a martial spirit in the bosoms of my countrymen, at a time when there is a general outcry against the prevalence of these dispositions. The British army, both by its skill and valour in the field, and by the discipline which rendered it, to the inhabitants of the several countries where its operations were carried on, a protection from the violence of their own troops, has performed services that will not allow the language of gratitude and admiration to be suppressed or restrained (whatever be the temper of the public mind) through a scrupulous dread lest the tribute due to the past should prove an injurious incentive for the future. Every man deserving the name of Briton adds his voice to the chorus which extols the exploits of his countrymen, with a consciousness, at times overpowering the effort, that they transcend all praise. — But this particular sentiment, thus irresistibly excited, is not sufficient. The nation would err grievously if she suffered the abuse which other states have made of military power to prevent her from perceiving that no people ever was or can be independent, free, or secure, much less great, in any sane application of the word, without a cultivation of military virtues. Nor let it be overlooked that the benefits derivable from these sources are placed within the reach of Great Britain,

under conditions peculiarly favourable. The same in-
sular position which, by rendering territorial incorpora-
tion impossible, utterly precludes the desire of conquest
under the most seductive shape it can assume, enables
her to rely, for her defence against foreign foes, chiefly
upon a species of armed force from which her own liber-
ties have nothing to fear. Such are the privileges of her
situation; and, by permitting, they invite her to give
way to the courageous instincts of human nature, and to
strengthen and refine them by culture.

But some have more than insinuated that a design
exists to subvert the civil character of the English people
by unconstitutional applications and unnecessary increase of military power. The advisers and abettors
of such a design, were it possible that it should exist,
would be guilty of the most heinous crime, which, upon
this planet, can be committed. Trusting that this apprehension arises from the delusive influences of an
honourable jealousy, let me hope that the martial
qualities which I venerate will be fostered by adhering to
those good old usages which experience has sanctioned,
and by availing ourselves of new means of indisputable
promise: particularly by applying, in its utmost possible extent, that system of tuition whose master-spring
is a habit of gradually enlightened subordination; —
by imparting knowledge, civil, moral, and religious,
in such measure that the mind, among all classes of
the community, may love, admire, and be prepared
and accomplished to defend, that country under whose

protection its faculties have been unfolded and its riches acquired; — by just dealing towards all orders of the state, so that, no members of it being trampled upon, courage may everywhere continue to rest immoveably upon its ancient English foundation, personal self-respect; — by adequate rewards and permanent honours conferred upon the deserving; — by encouraging athletic exercises and manly sports among the peasantry of the country; — and by especial care to provide and support institutions in which, during a time of peace, a reasonable proportion of the youth of the country may be instructed in military science.

I have only to add that I should feel little satisfaction in giving to the world these limited attempts to celebrate the virtues of my country, if I did not encourage a hope that a subject, which it has fallen within my province to treat only in the mass, will by other poets be illustrated in that detail which its importance calls for, and which will allow opportunities to give the merited applause to PERSONS as well as to THINGS.

The ode was published along with other pieces, now interspersed through this volume.

2.   "Discipline the rule whereof is passion."

LORD BROOKE.

3. The event is thus recorded in the journals of the day: "When the Austrians took Hochheim, in one part of the engagement they got to the brow of the hill, whence they had their first view of the Rhine. They instantly halted — not a gun was fired — not a voice heard: they

stood gazing on the river with those feelings which the events of the last fifteen years at once called up. Prince Schwartzenberg rode up to know the cause of this sudden stop; they then gave three cheers, rushed after the enemy, and drove them into the water."

4. See Filicaia's Ode.

5.   "From all the world's encumbrance did himself assoil."
                                            SPENSER.

6. The multiplication of mountain-ridges, described at the commencement of the third Stanza of this Ode as a kind of Jacob's Ladder leading to Heaven, is produced either by watery vapours, or sunny haze; — in the present instance by the latter cause. Allusions to the Ode entitled "Intimations of Immortality" pervade the last stanza of the foregoing Poem.

7. In these lines I am under obligation to the exquisite picture of "Jacob's Dream," by Mr. Allston, now in America. It is pleasant to make this public acknowledgment to a man of genius, whom I have the honour to rank among my friends.

8. Waters (as Mr. Westall informs us in the letter-press prefixed to his admirable views) are invariably found to flow through these caverns.

9. See the Phædon of Plato, by which this sonnet was suggested.

10. Wallachia is the country alluded to.

11. If in this sonnet I should seem to have borne a little too hard upon the personal appearance of the worthy Poissards of Calais, let me take shelter under

the authority of my lamented friend, the late Sir George
Beaumont. He, a most accurate observer, used to say
of them, that their features and countenances seemed
to have conformed to those of the creatures they dealt
in; at all events the resemblance was striking.

12. This is not the first poetical tribute which in our
times has been paid to this beautiful city. Mr. Southey,
in the "Poet's Pilgrimage," speaks of it in lines which
I cannot deny myself the pleasure of connecting with
my own.

> "Time hath not wronged her, nor hath ruin sought
>   Rudely her splendid structures to destroy,
> Save in those recent days, with evil fraught,
>   When mutability, in drunken joy
> Triumphant, and from all restraint released,
> Let loose her fierce and many-headed beast.
>
> "But for the scars in that unhappy rage
>   Inflicted, firm she stands and undecayed;
> Like our first Sires, a beautiful old age
>   Is hers in venerable years arrayed;
> And yet, to her, benignant stars may bring,
> What fate denies to man, — a second spring.
>
> "When I may read of tilts in days of old,
>   And tourneys graced by Chieftains of renown,
> Fair dames, grave citizens, and warriors bold,
>   If fancy would pourtray some stately town,
> Which for such pomp fit theatre should be,
> Fair Brugès, I shall then remember thee."

In this city are many vestiges of the splendour of the
Burgundian Dukedom, and the long black mantle universally worn by the females is probably a remnant of

the old Spanish connection, which, if I do not much deceive myself, is traceable in the grave deportment of its inhabitants. Brugès is comparatively little disturbed by that curious contest, or rather conflict, of Flemish with French propensities in matters of taste, so conspicuous through other parts of Flanders. The hotel to which we drove at Ghent furnished an odd instance. In the passages were paintings and statues, after the antique of Hebe and Apollo; and in the garden a little pond, about a yard and a half in diameter, with a weeping willow bending over it, and under the shade of that tree, in the centre of the pond, a wooden painted statue of a Dutch or Flemish boor, looking ineffably tender upon his mistress, and embracing her. A living duck, tethered at the feet of the sculptured lovers, alternately tormented a miserable eel and itself with endeavours to escape from its bonds and prison. Had we chanced to espy the hostess of the hotel in this quaint rural retreat, the exhibition would have been complete. She was a true Flemish figure, in the dress of the days of Holbein; her symbol of office, a weighty bunch of keys, pendent from her portly waist. In Brussels the modern taste in costume, architecture, etc., has got the mastery; in Ghent there is a struggle; but in Brugès old images are still paramount, and an air of monastic life among the quiet goings-on of a thinly-peopled city is inexpressibly soothing; a pensive grace seems to be cast over all, even the very children. — *Extract from Journal.*

13. "Let a wall of rocks be imagined from three to six hundred feet in height, and rising between France and Spain, so as physically to separate the two kingdoms — let us fancy this wall curved like a crescent, with its convexity towards France. Lastly, let us suppose, that in the very middle of the wall, a breach of 300 feet wide has been beaten down by the famous *Roland*, and we may have a good idea of what the mountaineers call the 'BRECHE DE ROLAND.'" — *Raymond's Pyrenees*.

14. See the beautiful Song in Mr. Coleridge's Tragedy, "The Remorse." Why is the harp of Quantock silent?

15. Before this quarter of the Black Forest was inhabited, the source of the Danube might have suggested some of those sublime images which Armstrong has so finely described; at present, the contrast is most striking. The Spring appears in a capacious stone Basin in front of a Ducal palace, with a pleasure-ground opposite; then, passing under the pavement, takes the form of a little, clear, bright, black, vigorous rill, barely wide enough to tempt the agility of a child five years old to leap over it, — and entering the garden, it joins, after a course of a few hundred yards, a stream much more considerable than itself. The *copiousness* of the spring at *Doneschingen* must have procured for it the honour of being named the Source of the Danube.

16. "The Staub-bach" is a narrow Stream, which, after a long course on the heights, comes to the sharp edge of a somewhat overhanging precipice, overleaps

it with a bound, and after a fall of 930 feet, forms again a rivulet. The vocal powers of these musical Beggars may seem to be exaggerated; but this wild and savage air was utterly unlike any sounds I had ever heard; the notes reached me from a distance, and on what occasion they were sung I could not guess, only they seemed to belong, in some way or other, to the Waterfall — and reminded me of religious services chanted to Streams and Fountains in Pagan times. Mr. Southey has thus accurately characterised the peculiarity of this music: "While we were at the Waterfall, some half-score peasants, chiefly women and girls, assembled just out of reach of the Spring, and set up — surely, the wildest chorus that ever was heard by human ears, — a song not of articulate sounds, but in which the voice was used as a mere instrument of music, more flexible than any which art could produce, — sweet, powerful, and thrilling beyond description." See Notes to *A Tale of Paraguay.*

17. The Convent whose site was pointed out, according to tradition, in this manner, is seated at its base. The architecture of the building is unimpressive, but the situation is worthy of the honour which the imagination of the mountaineers has conferred upon it.

18. Mount Righi.

19. Nearly 500 years (says Ebel, speaking of the French Invasion) had elapsed, when, for the first time, foreign soldiers were seen upon the frontiers of this small Canton, to impose upon it the laws of their governors.

20. Arnold Winkelried, at the battle of Sempach, broke an Austrian phalanx in this manner. The event is one of the most famous in the annals of Swiss heroism; and pictures and prints of it are frequent throughout the country.

21. This picture of the Last Supper has not only been grievously injured by time, but the greatest part of it, if not the whole, is said to have been retouched, or painted over again. These niceties may be left to connoisseurs, — I speak of it as I felt. The copy exhibited in London some years ago, and the engraving by Merghen, are both admirable; but in the original is a power which neither of those works has attained, or even approached.

22. The statues ranged round the spire and along the roof of the Cathedral of Milan have been found fault with by persons whose exclusive taste is unfortunate for themselves. It is true that the same expense and labour, judiciously directed to purposes more strictly architectural, might have much heightened the general effect of the building; for, seen from the ground, the Statues appear diminutive. But the *coup-d'œil*, from the best point of view, which is half way up the spire, must strike the unprejudiced person with admiration; and surely the selection and arrangement of the Figures is exquisitely fitted to support the religion of the country in the imaginations and feelings of the spectator. It was with great pleasure that I saw, during the two ascents which we made, several children, of different ages, tripping up and down the slender spire, and pausing to

look around them, with feelings much more animated than could have been derived from these or the finest works of art, if placed within easy reach. — Remember also that you have the Alps on one side, and on the other the Apennines, with the plain of Lombardy between!

23. Above the highest circle of figures is a zone of metallic stars.

24. See address to a Highland Girl, vol. iv, p. 143.

25. This Procession is a part of the sacramental service performed once a month. In the valley of Engelberg we had the good fortune to be present at the *Grand Festival* of the Virgin — but the Procession on that day, though consisting of upwards of 1000 persons, assembled from all the branches of the sequestered valley, was much less striking (notwithstanding the sublimity of the surrounding scenery); it wanted both the simplicity of the other and the accompaniment of the Glacier-columns, whose sisterly resemblance to the *moving* Figures gave it a most beautiful and solemn peculiarity.

26. Mount Righi, — Regina Montium.

27. The persuasion here expressed was not groundless. The first human consolation that the afflicted mother felt, was derived from this tribute to her son's memory, a fact which the author learned, at his own residence, from her daughter, who visited Europe some years afterward.

28. Near the town of Boulogne, and overhanging the beach, are the remains of a tower which bears the

name of Caligula, who here terminated his western expedition, of which these sea-shells were the boasted spoils. And at no great distance from these ruins, Buonaparte, standing upon a mound of earth, harangued his "Army of England," reminding them of the exploits of Cæsar, and pointing towards the white cliffs, upon which their standards *were to float*. He recommended also a subscription to be raised among the Soldiery to erect on that ground, in memory of the foundation of the "Legion of Honour," a Column — which was not completed at the time we were there.

29. This is a most grateful sight for an Englishman returning to his native land. Everywhere one misses in the cultivated grounds abroad, the animated and soothing accompaniment of animals ranging and selecting their own food at will.

30. At the head of the Valais. Les Fourches, the point at which the two chains of mountains part, that inclose the Valais, which terminates at St. Maurice.

31. Sarnen, one of the two capitals of the Canton of Unterwalden; the spot here alluded to is close to the town, and is called the Landenberg, from the tyrant of that name, whose château formerly stood there. On the 1st of January 1308, the great day which the confederated Heroes had chosen for the deliverance of their country, all the castles of the Governors were taken by force or stratagem; and the Tyrants themselves conducted, with their creatures, to the frontiers, after having witnessed the destruction of their strongholds.

From that time the Landenberg has been the place where the Legislators of this division of the Canton assemble. The site, which is well described by Ebel, is one of the most beautiful in Switzerland.

32. The bridges of Lucerne are roofed, and open at the sides, so that the passenger has, at the same time, the benefit of shade, and a view of the magnificent country. The pictures are attached to the rafters; those from Scripture History, on the Cathedral-bridge, amount, according to my notes, to 240. Subjects from the Old Testament face the passenger as he goes towards the Cathedral, and those from the New as he returns. The pictures on these bridges, as well as those in most other parts of Switzerland, are not to be spoken of as works of art; but they are instruments admirably answering the purpose for which they were designed.

34. A Poet, whose works are not yet known as they deserve to be, thus enters upon his description of the "Ruins of Rome": —

> "The rising Sun
> Flames on the ruins in the purer air
> Towering aloft";

and ends thus —

> "The setting Sun displays
> His visible great round, between yon towers,
> As through two shady cliffs."

Mr. Crowe, in his excellent loco-descriptive Poem, "Lewesdon Hill," is still more expeditious, finishing the whole on a May-morning, before breakfast.

[219]

"To-morrow for severer thought, but now
To breakfast, and keep festival to-day."

No one believes, or is desired to believe, that those
Poems were actually composed within such limits of
time; nor was there any reason why a prose statement
should acquaint the reader with the plain fact, to the
disturbance of poetic credibility. But, in the present
case, I am compelled to mention, that this series of
Sonnets was the growth of many years; — the one
which stands the 14th was the first produced; and
others were added upon occasional visits to the Stream,
or as recollections of the scenes upon its banks awakened
a wish to describe them. In this manner I had proceeded insensibly, without perceiving that I was tres-
passing upon ground pre-occupied, at least as far as
intention went, by Mr. Coleridge; who, more than
twenty years ago, used to speak of writing a rural Poem,
to be entitled "The Brook," of which he has given a
sketch in a recent publication. But a particular subject cannot, I think, much interfere with a general one;
and I have been further kept from encroaching upon
any right Mr. C. may still wish to exercise, by the restriction which the frame of the Sonnet imposed upon
me, narrowing unavoidably the range of thought, and
precluding, though not without its advantages, many
graces to which a freer movement of verse would naturally have led.

May I not venture, then, to hope, that, instead of
being a hindrance by anticipation of any part of the

subject, these Sonnets may remind Mr. Coleridge of his own more comprehensive design, and induce him to fulfil it? —— There is a sympathy in streams, — "one calleth to another"; and I would gladly believe, that "The Brook" will, ere long, murmur in concert with "The Duddon." But, asking pardon for this fancy, I need not scruple to say that those verses must indeed be ill-fated which can enter upon such pleasant walks of nature without receiving and giving inspiration. The power of waters over the minds of Poets has been acknowledged from the earliest ages; — through the "Flumina amem sylvasque inglorius" of Virgil, down to the sublime apostrophe to the great rivers of the earth by Armstrong, and the simple ejaculation of Burns (chosen, if I recollect right, by Mr. Coleridge, as a motto for his embryo "Brook").

> "The Muse nae Poet ever fand her,
>   Till by himsel' he learned to wander,
>   Adown some trotting burn's meander,
>   AND NA' THINK LANG."

34. The deer alluded to is the Leigh, a gigantic species long since extinct.

35. These two lines are in a great measure taken from "The Beauties of Spring, a Juvenile Poem," by the Rev. Joseph Sympson. He was a native of Cumberland, and was educated at Hawkshead school: his poems are little known, but they contain passages of splendid description; and the versification of his "Vision of Alfred" is harmonious and animated. In describing

the motions of the Sylphs that constitute the strange machinery of his Poem, he uses the following illustrative simile:

"Glancing from their plumes
A changeful light the azure vault illumes.
Less varying hues beneath the Pole adorn
The streamy glories of the Boreal morn,
That wavering to and fro their radiance shed
On Bothnia's gulf with glassy ice o'erspread.
Where the lone native, as he homeward glides,
On polished sandals o'er the imprisoned tides,
And still the balance of his frame preserves,
Wheeled on alternate foot in lengthening curves,
Sees at a glance, above him and below,
Two rival heavens with equal splendour glow.
Sphered in the centre of the world he seems;
For all around with soft effulgence gleams;
Stars, moons, and meteors, ray opposed to ray,
And solemn midnight pours the blaze of day."

He was a man of ardent feeling, and his faculties of mind, particularly his memory, were extraordinary. Brief notices of his life ought to find a place in the History of Westmoreland.

36. See Humboldt's *Personal Narrative*.

37. [Note on Sonnets XVII and XVIII.] The Eagle requires a large domain for its support: but several pairs, not many years ago, were constantly resident in this country, building their nests in the steeps of Borrowdale, Wastdale, Ennerdale, and on the eastern side of Helvellyn. Often have I heard anglers speak of the grandeur of their appearance, as they hovered over

Red Tarn, in one of the coves of this mountain. The bird frequently returns, but is always destroyed. Not long since, one visited Rydal lake, and remained some hours near its banks; the consternation which it occasioned among the different species of fowl, particularly the herons, was expressed by loud screams. The horse also is naturally afraid of the eagle. — There were several Roman stations among these mountains; the most considerable seems to have been in a meadow at the head of Windermere, established, undoubtedly, as a check over the passes of Kirkstone, Dunmail-raise, and of Hardknot and Wrynose. On the margin of Rydal lake, a coin of Trajan was discovered very lately. — The Roman Fort here alluded to, called by the country people *"Hardknot Castle,"* is most impressively situated half-way down the hill on the right of the road that descends from Hardknot into Eskdale. It has escaped the notice of most antiquarians, and is but slightly mentioned by Lysons. — The Druidical Circle is about half a mile to the left of the road ascending Stoneside from the vale of Duddon: the country people call it *"Sunken Church."*

The reader who may have been interested in the foregoing Sonnets (which together may be considered as a Poem) will not be displeased to find in this place a prose account of the Duddon, extracted from Green's comprehensive *Guide to the Lakes*, lately published. "The road leading from Coniston to Broughton is over high ground, and commands a view of the River Duddon;

which, at high water, is a grand sight, having the beautiful and fertile lands of Lancashire and Cumberland stretching each way from its margin. In this extensive view, the face of nature is displayed in a wonderful variety of hill and dale, wooded grounds and buildings; amongst the latter Broughton Tower, seated on the crown of a hill, rising elegantly from the valley, is an object of extraordinary interest. Fertility on each side is gradually diminished, and lost in the superior heights of Backcomb, in Cumberland, and the high lands between Kirkby and Ulverstone.

"The road from Broughton to Seathwaite is on the banks of the Duddon, and on its Lancashire side it is of various elevations. The river is an amusing companion, one while brawling and tumbling over rocky precipices, until the agitated water becomes again calm by arriving at a smoother and less precipitous bed, but its course is soon again ruffled, and the current thrown into every variety of foam which the rocky channel of a river can give to water." — *Vide* Green's *Guide to the Lakes*, vol. i. pp. 98–100.

After all, the traveller would be most gratified who should approach this beautiful Stream, neither at its source, as is done in the Sonnets, nor from its termination; but from Coniston over Walna Scar; first descending into a little circular valley, a collateral compartment of the long winding vale through which flows the Duddon. This recess, towards the close of September, when the after-grass of the meadows is still of a fresh green, with

the leaves of many of the trees faded, but perhaps none
fallen, is truly enchanting. At a point elevated enough
to show the various objects in the valley, and not so
high as to diminish their importance, the stranger will
instinctively halt. On the foreground, a little below the
most favourable station, a rude foot-bridge is thrown
over the bed of the noisy brook foaming by the wayside.
Russet and craggy hills, of bold and varied outline,
surround the level valley, which is besprinkled with grey
rocks plumed with birch trees. A few homesteads are
interspersed, in some places peeping out from among
the rocks like hermitages, whose site has been chosen
for the benefit of sunshine as well as shelter; in other
instances, the dwelling-house, barn, and byre, compose
together a cruciform structure, which, with its embower-
ing trees, and the ivy clothing part of the walls and roof
like a fleece, call to mind the remains of an ancient abbey.
Time, in most cases, and nature everywhere, have given
a sanctity to the humble works of man that are scattered over this peaceful retirement. Hence a harmony
of tone and colour, a consummation and perfection of
beauty, which would have been marred had aim or purpose interfered with the course of convenience, utility,
or necessity. This unvitiated region stands in no need of
the veil of twilight to soften or disguise its features. As
it glistens in the morning sunshine, it would fill the
spectator's heart with gladsomeness. Looking from our
chosen station, he would feel an impatience to rove
among its pathways, to be greeted by the milkmaid,

to wander from house to house exchanging "good-morrows" as he passed the open doors; but, at evening, when the sun is set, and a pearly light gleams from the western quarter of the sky, with an answering light from the smooth surface of the meadows; when the trees are dusky, but each kind still distinguishable; when the cool air has condensed the blue smoke rising from the cottage chimneys; when the dark mossy stones seem to sleep in the bed of the foaming brook; *then* he would be unwilling to move forward, not less from a reluctance to relinquish what he beholds, than from an apprehension of disturbing, by his approach, the quietness beneath him. Issuing from the plain of this valley, the brook descends in a rapid torrent passing by the churchyard of Seathwaite. The traveller is thus conducted at once into the midst of the wild and beautiful scenery which gave occasion to the Sonnets from the 14th to the 20th inclusive. From the point where the Seathwaite brook joins the Duddon is a view upwards into the pass through which the river makes its way into the plain of Donnerdale. The perpendicular rock on the right bears the ancient British name of The Pen; the one opposite is called Wallabarrow Crag, a name that occurs in other places to designate rocks of the same character. The *chaotic* aspect of the scene is well marked by the expression of a stranger, who strolled out while dinner was preparing, and at his return, being asked by his host, "What way he had been wandering?" replied, "As far as it is *finished!*"

The bed of the Duddon is here strewn with large fragments of rocks fallen from aloft; which, as Mr. Green truly says, "are happily adapted to the many-shaped waterfalls" (or rather water-breaks, for none of them are high) "displayed in the short space of half a mile." That there is some hazard in frequenting these desolate places, I myself have had proof; for one night an immense mass of rock fell upon the very spot where, with a friend, I had lingered the day before. "The concussion," says Mr. Green, speaking of the event (for he also, in the practice of his art, on that day sat exposed for a still longer time to the same peril), "was heard, not without alarm, by the neighbouring shepherds." But to return to Seathwaite Churchyard: it contains the following inscription: —

"In memory of the Reverend Robert Walker, who died the 25th of June 1802, in the 93d year of his age, and 67th of his curacy at Seathwaite.

"Also, of Anne his wife, who died the 28th of January, in the 93d year of her age."

In the parish-register of Seathwaite Chapel is this notice: —

"Buried, June 28th, the Rev. Robert Walker. He was curate of Seathwaite sixty-six years. He was a man singular for his temperance, industry, and integrity."

This individual is the Pastor alluded to, in the 18th Sonnet, as a worthy compeer of the country parson of Chaucer, etc. In the seventh book of "The Excursion," an abstract of his character is given, beginning, —

"A Priest abides before whose life such doubts
Fall to the ground; —"

and some account of his life, for it is worthy of being
recorded, will not be out of place here.

MEMOIR OF THE REVEREND ROBERT WALKER

In the year 1709, Robert Walker was born at Under-
crag, in Seathwaite; he was the youngest of twelve
children. His eldest brother, who inherited the small
family estate, died at Under-crag, aged ninety-four,
being twenty-four years older than the subject of this
memoir, who was born of the same mother. Robert was
a sickly infant; and, through his boyhood and youth,
continuing to be of delicate frame and tender health,
it was deemed best, according to the country phrase,
to *breed him a scholar;* for it was not likely that he would
be able to earn a livelihood by bodily labour. At that
period few of these dales were furnished with school-
houses; the children being taught to read and write
in the chapel; and in the same consecrated building,
where he officiated for so many years both as preacher
and schoolmaster, he himself received the rudiments of
his education. In his youth he became schoolmaster at
Loweswater; not being called upon, probably, in that
situation to teach more than reading, writing, and
arithmetic. But, by the assistance of a "Gentleman"
in the neighbourhood, he acquired, at leisure hours, a
knowledge of the classics, and became qualified for tak-

ing holy orders. Upon his ordination, he had the offer
of two curacies: the one, Torver, in the vale of Coniston, — the other, Seathwaite, in his native vale. The
value of each was the same, viz., five pounds *per
annum;* but the cure of Seathwaite having a cottage
attached to it, as he wished to marry, he chose it in
preference. The young person on whom his affections
were fixed, though in the condition of a domestic servant, had given promise, by her serious and modest
deportment, and by her virtuous dispositions, that she
was worthy to become the helpmeet of a man entering
upon a plan of life such as he had marked out for himself. By her frugality she had stored up a small sum
of money, with which they began housekeeping. In
1735 or 1736, he entered upon his curacy; and, nineteen
years afterwards, his situation is thus described, in some
letters to be found in the Annual Register for 1760,
from which the following is extracted: —

"To Mr. ——

"Coniston, July 26, 1754.

"Sir — I was the other day upon a party of pleasure,
about five or six miles from this place, where I met with
a very striking object, and of a nature not very common.
Going into a clergyman's house (of whom I had frequently heard), I found him sitting at the head of a
long square table, such as is commonly used in this
country by the lower class of people, dressed in a coarse
blue frock, trimmed with black horn buttons; a checked

shirt, a leathern strap about his neck for a stock, a coarse apron, and a pair of great wooden-soled shoes plated with iron to preserve them (that we call clogs in these parts), with a child upon his knee, eating his breakfast; his wife, and the remainder of his children, were some of them employed in waiting upon each other, the rest in teasing and spinning wool, at which trade he is a great proficient; and moreover, when it is made ready for sale, will lay it, by sixteen or thirty-two pounds' weight, upon his back, and on foot, seven or eight miles, will carry it to the market, even in the depth of winter. I was not much surprised at all this, as you may possibly be, having heard a great deal of it related before. But I must confess myself astonished with the alacrity and the good humour that appeared both in the clergyman and his wife, and more so at the sense and ingenuity of the clergyman himself. . . ."

Then follows a letter from another person, dated 1755, from which an extract shall be given: —

"By his frugality and good management he keeps the wolf from the door, as we say; and if he advances a little in the world, it is owing more to his own care than to anything else he has to rely upon. I don't find his inclination is running after further preferment. He is settled among the people, that are happy among themselves; and lives in the greatest unanimity and friendship with them; and, I believe, the minister and people are exceedingly satisfied with each other; and indeed how should they be dissatisfied when they have a person of so much worth and probity for their pastor? A man who, for his candour and meekness, his sober, chaste, and virtuous conversation, his soundness in principle and practice, is an ornament to his profession, and an honour to the country he is in; and bear with me if I say, the plainness of his dress, the sanctity of his manners, the simplicity of his doctrine, and the vehemence of his expression, have a sort of resemblance to the pure practice of primitive Christianity."

We will now give his own account of himself, to be found in the same place.

FROM THE REVEREND ROBERT WALKER

"Sir — Yours of the 26th instant was communicated to me by Mr. C——, and I should have returned an immediate answer, but the hand of Providence, then laying heavy upon an amiable pledge of conjugal endearment, hath since taken from me a promising girl, which the disconsolate mother too pensively laments the loss of; though we have yet eight living, all healthful, hopeful children, whose names and ages are as follows: Zaccheus, aged almost eighteen years; Elizabeth, sixteen years and ten months; Mary, fifteen; Moses, thirteen years and three months; Sarah, ten years and three months; Mabel, eight years and three months; William Tyson, three years and eight months; and Anne Esther, one year and three months; besides

Anne, who died two years and six months ago, and was then aged between nine and ten; and Eleanor, who died the 23d inst., January, aged six years and ten months. Zaccheus, the eldest child, is now learning the trade of a tanner, and has two years and a half of his apprenticeship to serve. The annual income of my chapel at present, as near as I can compute it, may amount to about 17*l*., of which is paid in cash, viz., 5*l*. from the bounty of Queen Anne, and 5*l*. from W. P., Esq., of P——, out of the annual rents, he being lord of the manor, and 3*l*. from the several inhabitants of L——, settled upon the tenements as a rent-charge; the house and gardens I value at 4*l*. yearly, and not worth more; and I believe the surplice fees and voluntary contributions, one year with another, may be worth 3*l*.; but as the inhabitants are few in number, and the fees very low, this last-mentioned sum consists merely in free-will offerings.

"I am situated greatly to my satisfaction with regard to the conduct and behaviour of my auditory, who not only live in the happy ignorance of the follies and vices of the age, but in mutual peace and goodwill with one another, and are seemingly (I hope really too) sincere Christians, and sound members of the established church, not one dissenter of any denomination being amongst them all. I got to the value of 40*l*. for my wife's fortune, but had no real estate of my own, being the youngest son of twelve children, born of obscure parents; and, though my income has been but small, and my family large, yet, by a providential blessing upon my own diligent endeavours, the kindness of friends, and a cheap country to live in, we have always had the necessaries of life. By what I have written (which is a true and exact account, to the best of my knowledge) I hope you will not think your favour to me out of the late worthy Dr. Stratford's effects quite misbestowed, for which I must ever gratefully own myself, Sir, your much obliged and most obedient humble servant.

"R. W., Curate of S——

"To Mr. C., of Lancaster."

About the time when this letter was written, the Bishop of Chester recommended the scheme of joining the curacy of Ulpha to the contiguous one of Seathwaite, and the nomination was offered to Mr. Walker; but an unexpected difficulty arising, Mr. W., in a letter to the Bishop (a copy of which, in his own beautiful handwriting, now lies before me), thus expresses himself. "If he," meaning the person in whom the difficulty originated, "had suggested any such objection before, I should utterly have declined any attempt to the curacy of Ulpha: indeed, I was always apprehensive it might be disagreeable to my auditory at Seathwaite, as they have been always accustomed to double duty, and the inhabitants of Ulpha despair of being able to support a schoolmaster who is not curate there also; which suppressed all thoughts in me of serving them both." And in a second letter to the Bishop he writes: —

"My Lord — I have the favour of yours of the 1st instant, and am exceedingly obliged on account of the Ulpha affair: if that curacy should lapse into your Lordship's hands, I would beg leave rather to decline than embrace it; for the chapels of Seathwaite and Ulpha, annexed together, would be apt to cause a general discontent among the inhabitants of both places; by either thinking themselves slighted, being only served alternately, or neglected in the duty, or attributing it to covetousness in me; all which occasions of murmuring I would willingly avoid."

And in concluding his former letter, he expresses a similar sentiment upon the same occasion, "desiring, if it be possible, however, as much as in me lieth, to live peaceably with all men."

The year following, the curacy of Seathwaite was again augmented; and, to effect this augmentation, fifty pounds had been advanced by himself; and, in 1760, lands were purchased with eight hundred pounds. Scanty as was his income, the frequent offer of much better benefices could not tempt Mr. W. to quit a situation where he had been so long happy, with a consciousness of being useful. Among his papers I find the following copy of a letter, dated 1775, twenty years after his refusal of the curacy of Ulpha, which will show what exertions had been made for one of his sons.

"MAY IT PLEASE YOUR GRACE — Our remote situation here makes it difficult to get the necessary information for transacting business regularly; such is the reason of my giving your Grace the present trouble.

"The bearer (my son) is desirous of offering himself candidate for deacon's orders at your Grace's ensuing ordination; the first, on the 25th instant, so that his papers could not be transmitted in due time. As he is now fully at age, and I have afforded him education to the utmost of my ability, it would give me great satisfaction (if your Grace would take him, and find him qualified) to have him ordained. His constitution has been tender for some years; he entered the college of Dublin, but his health would not permit him to continue there, or I would have supported him much longer. He has been with me at home above a year, in which time he has gained great strength of body, sufficient, I hope, to enable him for performing the function. Divine Providence, assisted by liberal benefactors, has blest my endeavours, from a small income, to rear a numerous family; and as my time of life renders me now unfit for much future expectancy from this world, I should be glad to see my son settled in a promising way to acquire an honest livelihood for himself. His behaviour, so far in life, has been irreproachable; and I hope he will not degenerate, in principles or practice, from the precepts and pattern of an indulgent parent. Your Grace's favourable reception of this, from a distant corner of the diocese, and an obscure hand, will excite filial gratitude,

and a due use shall be made of the obligation vouch-
safed thereby to your Grace's very dutiful and most
obedient Son and Servant,

"ROBERT WALKER."

The same man, who was thus liberal in the education
of his numerous family, was even munificent in hospi-
tality as a parish priest. Every Sunday were served
upon the long table, at which he has been described
sitting with a child upon his knee, messes of broth for
the refreshment of those of his congregation who came
from a distance, and usually took their seats as parts of
his own household. It seems scarcely possible that this
custom could have commenced before the augmentation of his cure; and what would to many have been
a high price of self-denial was paid, by the pastor and
his family, for this gratification; as the treat could only
be provided by dressing at one time the whole, perhaps,
of their weekly allowance of fresh animal food; consequently, for a succession of days, the table was covered
with cold victuals only. His generosity in old age may
be still further illustrated by a little circumstance relating to an orphan grandson, then ten years of age,
which I find in a copy of a letter to one of his sons; he
requests that half a guinea may be left for "little
Robert's pocket-money," who was then at school: in-
trusting it to the care of a lady, who, as he says, "may
sometimes frustrate his squandering it away foolishly,"
and promising to send him an equal allowance annually

for the same purpose. The conclusion of the same letter is so characteristic, that I cannot forbear to transcribe it. "We," meaning his wife and himself, "are in our wonted state of health, allowing for the hasty strides of old age knocking daily at our door, and threateningly telling us we are not only mortal, but must expect ere long to take our leave of our ancient cottage, and lie down in our last dormitory. Pray pardon my neglect to answer yours: let us hear sooner from you, to augment the mirth of the Christmas holidays. Wishing you all the pleasures of the approaching season, I am, dear Son, with lasting sincerity, yours affectionately,

"ROBERT WALKER."

He loved old customs and old usages, and in some instances stuck to them to his own loss; for, having had a sum of money lodged in the hands of a neighbouring tradesman, when long course of time had raised the rate of interest, and more was offered, he refused to accept it; an act not difficult to one, who, while he was drawing seventeen pounds a year from his curacy, declined, as we have seen, to add the profits of another small benefice to his own, lest he should be suspected of cupidity. From this vice he was utterly free; he made no charge for teaching school; such as could afford to pay gave him what they pleased. When very young, having kept a diary of his expenses, however trifling, the large amount, at the end of the year, surprised him; and from that time the rule of his life was to be econom-

ical, not avaricious. At his decease he left behind him
no less a sum than 2000*l.*; and such a sense of his various
excellences was prevalent in the country, that the epithet of WONDERFUL is to this day attached to his name.

There is in the above sketch something so extraordinary as to require further *explanatory* details. And
to begin with his industry; eight hours in each day,
during five days of the week, and half of Saturday,
except when the labours of husbandry were urgent, he
was occupied in teaching. His seat was within the rails
of the altar; the communion table was his desk; and
like Shenstone's schoolmistress, the master employed
himself at the spinning-wheel, while the children were
repeating their lessons by his side. Every evening, after
school hours, if not more profitably engaged, he continued the same kind of labour, exchanging, for the
benefit of exercise, the small wheel, at which he had
sate, for the large one on which wool is spun, the
spinner stepping to and fro. Thus was the wheel constantly in readiness to prevent the waste of a moment's
time. Nor was his industry with the pen, when occasion called for it, less eager. Intrusted with extensive
management of public and private affairs, he acted, in
his rustic neighbourhood, as scrivener, writing out
petitions, deeds of conveyance, wills, covenants, etc.,
with pecuniary gain to himself, and to the great benefit of his employers. These labours (at all times considerable) at one period of the year, viz., between Christmas
and Candlemas, when money transactions are settled

in this country, were often so intense, that he passed
great part of the night, and sometimes whole nights, at
his desk. His garden also was tilled by his own hand;
he had a right of pasturage upon the mountains for a
few sheep and a couple of cows, which required his attendance; with this pastoral occupation he joined the
labours of husbandry upon a small scale, renting two
or three acres in addition to his own less than one acre
of glebe; and the humblest drudgery which the cultivation of these fields required was performed by himself.

He also assisted his neighbours in hay-making and
shearing their flocks, and in the performance of this
latter service he was eminently dexterous. They, in
their turn, complimented him with the present of a
haycock, or a fleece; less as a recompence for this particular service than as a general acknowledgment. The
Sabbath was in a strict sense kept holy; the Sunday
evenings being devoted to reading the Scripture and
family prayer. The principal festivals appointed by the
Church were also duly observed; but through every
other day in the week, through every week in the year,
he was incessantly occupied in work of hand or mind;
not allowing a moment for recreation, except upon a
Saturday afternoon, when he indulged himself with a
Newspaper, or sometimes with a Magazine. The frugality and temperance established in his house were as
admirable as the industry. Nothing to which the name
of luxury could be given was there known; in the latter
part of his life, indeed, when tea had been brought into

almost general use, it was provided for visitors, and for such of his own family as returned occasionally to his roof, and had been accustomed to this refreshment elsewhere; but neither he nor his wife ever partook of it. The raiment worn by his family was comely and decent, but as simple as their diet; the home-spun materials were made up into apparel by their own hands. At the time of the decease of this thrifty pair, their cottage contained a large store of webs of woollen and linen cloth, woven from thread of their own spinning. And it is remarkable that the pew in the chapel in which the family used to sit, remains neatly lined with woollen cloth spun by the pastor's own hands. It is the only pew in the chapel so distinguished; and I know of no other instance of his conformity to the delicate accommodations of modern times. The fuel of the house, like that of their neighbours, consisted of peat, procured from the mosses by their own labour. The lights by which, in the winter evenings, their work was performed, were of their own manufacture, such as still continue to be used in these cottages; they are made of the pith of rushes dipped in any unctuous substance that the house affords. *White* candles, as tallow candles are here called, were reserved to honour the Christmas festivals, and were perhaps produced upon no other occasions. Once a month, during the proper season, a sheep was drawn from their small mountain flock, and killed for the use of the family; and a cow, towards the close of the year, was salted and dried for winter provision; the hide was tanned to furnish them with shoes. — By these various resources, this venerable clergyman reared a numerous family, not only preserving them, as he affectingly says, "from wanting the necessaries of life"; but affording them an unstinted education, and the means of raising themselves in society. In this they were eminently assisted by the effects of their father's example, his precepts, and injunctions: he was aware that truth-speaking, as a moral virtue, is best secured by inculcating attention to accuracy of report even on trivial occasions; and so rigid were the rules of honesty by which he endeavoured to bring up his family, that if one of them had chanced to find in the lanes or fields anything of the least use or value without being able to ascertain to whom it belonged, he always insisted upon the child's carrying it back to the place from which it had been brought.

No one, it might be thought, could, as has been described, convert his body into a machine, as it were, of industry for the humblest uses, and keep his thoughts so frequently bent upon secular concerns, without grievous injury to the more precious parts of his nature. How could the powers of intellect thrive, or its graces be displayed, in the midst of circumstances apparently so unfavourable, and where, to the direct cultivation of the mind, so small a portion of time was allotted? But, in this extraordinary man, things in their nature adverse were reconciled. His converation was remarkable, not only for being chaste and pure, but for the degree in which it was fervent and eloquent; his written style was correct, simple, and animated. Nor did his *affections* suffer more than his intellect; he was tenderly alive to all the duties of his pastoral office: the poor and needy "he never sent empty away," — the stranger was fed and refreshed in passing that unfrequented vale — the sick were visited; and the feelings of humanity found further exercise among the distresses and embarrassments in the worldly estate of his neighbours, with which his talents for business made him acquainted; and the disinterestedness, impartiality, and uprightness which he maintained in the management of all affairs confided to him were virtues seldom separated in his own conscience from religious obligation. Nor could such conduct fail to remind those who witnessed it of a spirit nobler than law or custom: they felt convictions which, but for such intercourse, could not have been afforded, that as in the practice of their pastor there was no guile, so in his faith there was nothing hollow; and we are warranted in believing that upon these occasions selfishness, obstinacy, and discord would often give way before the breathings of his good-will and saintly integrity. It may be presumed also — while his humble congregation were listening to the moral precepts which he delivered from the pulpit, and to the Christian exhortations that they should love their neighbours as themselves, and do as they would be done unto — that peculiar efficacy was given to the preacher's labours by recollections in the minds of his congregation that they were called upon to do no more than his own actions were daily setting before their eyes.

The afternoon service in the chapel was less numerously attended than that of the morning, but by a more serious auditory; the lesson from the New Testament, on those occasions, was accompanied by Burkitt's Commentaries. These lessons he read with impassioned emphasis, frequently drawing tears from his hearers, and leaving a lasting impression upon their minds. His devotional feelings and the powers of his own mind were further exercised, along with those of his family, in perusing the Scriptures: not only on the Sunday evenings, but on every other evening, while the rest of the household were at work, some one of the children, and in her turn the servant, for the sake of practice in reading, or for instruction, read the Bible aloud; and in this manner the whole was repeatedly gone through. That no common importance was attached to the observance of religious ordinances by his family, appears from the following memorandum by one of his descendants, which I am tempted to insert at length, as it is characteristic and somewhat curious. "There is a small chapel in the county palatine of Lancaster, where a certain clergyman has regularly officiated above sixty years, and a few months ago administered the sacrament of the Lord's Supper in the same, to a decent number of devout communicants. After the clergyman had received himself, the first company out of the assembly who approached the altar, and kneeled down to be partakers of the sacred elements, consisted of the parson's wife, to whom he had been married upwards of sixty years; one son and his wife; four daughters, each with her husband; whose ages, all added together, amount to above 714 years. The several and respective distances from the place of each of their abodes to the chapel where they all communicated, will measure more than 1000 English miles. Though the narration will appear surprising, it is without doubt a fact that the same persons, exactly four years before, met at the same place, and all joined in performance of the same venerable duty."

He was indeed most zealously attached to the doctrine and frame of the Established Church. We have seen him congratulating himself that he had no dissenters in his cure of any denomination. Some allowance must be made for the state of opinion when his first religious impressions were received, before the reader will acquit him of bigotry, when I mention that at the time of the augmentation of the cure, he refused to invest part of the money in the purchase of an estate offered to him upon advantageous terms, because the proprietor was a quaker; — whether from scrupulous apprehension that a blessing would not attend a contract framed for the benefit of the church between persons not in religious sympathy with each other; or, as a seeker of peace, he was afraid of the uncomplying disposition which at one time was too frequently conspicuous in that sect. Of this an instance had fallen under his own notice; for,

while he taught school at Loweswater, certain persons
of that denomination had refused to pay annual interest
due under the title of Church-stock;[1] a great hardship
upon the incumbent, for the curacy of Loweswater
was then scarcely less poor than that of Seathwaite.
To what degree this prejudice of his was blameable need
not be determined; — certain it is, that he was not
only desirous, as he himself says, to live in peace, but
in love, with all men. He was placable, and charitable
in his judgments; and, however correct in conduct
and rigorous to himself, he was ever ready to forgive
the trespasses of others, and to soften the censure that
was cast upon their frailties. — It would be unpardon-
able to omit that, in the maintenance of his virtues,
he received due support from the partner of his long life.
She was equally strict, in attending to her share of their
joint cares, nor less diligent in her appropriate occupations. A person who had been some time their servant
in the latter part of their lives, concluded the pane-
gyric of her mistress by saying to me, "She was no less
excellent than her husband; she was good to the poor;
she was good to everything!" He survived for a short
time this virtuous companion. When she died, he ordered
that her body should be borne to the grave by three of
her daughters and one granddaughter; and, when the
corpse was lifted from the threshold, he insisted upon

[1] Mr. Walker's charity being of that kind which "seeketh not
her own," he would rather forego his rights than distrain for dues
which the parties liable refused, as a point of conscience, to pay.

lending his aid, and feeling about, for he was then almost blind, took hold of a napkin fixed to the coffin;
and, as a bearer of the body, entered the chapel, a few
steps from the lowly parsonage.

What a contrast does the life of this obscurely-seated,
and, in point of worldly wealth, poorly-repaid Church-
man, present to that of a Cardinal Wolsey!

> "O 't is a burthen, Cromwell, 't is a burthen
> Too heavy for a man who hopes for heaven!"

We have been dwelling upon images of peace in the
moral world, that have brought us again to the quiet
enclosure of consecrated ground in which this venerable pair lie interred. The sounding brook, that rolls
close by the churchyard, without disturbing feeling or
meditation, is now unfortunately laid bare; but not
long ago it participated, with the chapel, the shade of
some stately ash-trees, which will not spring again.
While the spectator from this spot is looking round
upon the girdle of stony mountains that encompasses
the vale, — masses of rock, out of which monuments for
all men that ever existed might have been hewn — it
would surprise him to be told, as with truth he might
be, that the plain blue slab dedicated to the memory of
this aged pair is a production of a quarry in North
Wales. It was sent as a mark of respect by one of their
descendants from the vale of Festiniog, a region almost
as beautiful as that in which it now lies!

Upon the Seathwaite Brook, at a small distance from
the parsonage, has been erected a mill for spinning yarn;

it is a mean and disagreeable object, though not unimportant to the spectator, as calling to mind the momentous changes wrought by such inventions in the frame of society — changes which have proved especially unfavourable to these mountain solitudes. So much had been effected by those new powers, before the subject of the preceding biographical sketch closed his life, that their operation could not escape his notice, and doubtless excited touching reflections upon the comparatively insignificant results of his own manual industry. But Robert Walker was not a man of times and circumstances; had he lived at a later period, the principal of duty would have produced application as unremitting; the same energy of character would have been displayed, though in many instances with widely different effects.

With pleasure I annex, as illustrative and confirmatory of the above account, extracts from a paper in the *Christian Remembrancer*, October 1819: it bears an assumed signature, but is known to be the work of the Rev. Robert Bamford, vicar of Bishopton, in the county of Durham; a great-grandson of Mr. Walker, whose worth it commemorates, by a record not the less valuable for being written in very early youth: —

"His house was a nursery of virtue. All the inmates were industrious, and cleanly, and happy. Sobriety, neatness, quietness, characterised the whole family. No railings, no idleness, no indulgence of passion were permitted. Every child, however young, had its appointed engagements; every hand was busy. Knitting, spinning, reading, writing, mending clothes, making shoes, were by the different children constantly performing. The father himself sitting amongst them and guiding their thoughts, was engaged in the same occupations. . . .

"He sate up late, and rose early; when the family were at rest, he retired to a little room which he had built on the roof of his house. He had slated it, and fitted it up with shelves for his books, his stock of cloth, wearing apparel, and his utensils. There many a cold winter's night, without fire, while the roof was glazed with ice, did he remain reading or writing till the day dawned. He taught the children in the chapel, for there was no school-house. Yet in that cold, damp place he never had a fire. He used to send the children in parties either to his own fire at home or make them run up the mountain-side.

. . . .

"It may be further mentioned, that he was a passionate admirer of Nature; she was his mother and he was a dutiful child. While engaged on the mountains, it was his greatest pleasure to view the rising sun; and in tranquil evenings, as it slided behind the hills, he blessed its departure. He was skilled in fossils and plants; a constant observer of the stars and winds: the atmosphere was his delight. He made many experiments on its nature and properties. In summer he used to gather a multitude of flies and insects, and, by his entertaining description, amuse and instruct his children. They shared all his daily employments, and derived many sentiments of love and benevolence from his observations on the works and productions of Nature. Whether they were following him in the field, or surrounding him in school, he took every opportunity of storing their minds with useful information. — Nor was the circle of his influence confined to Seathwaite. Many a distant mother has told her child of Mr. Walker, and begged him to be as good a man.

.   .   .   .

"Once, when I was very young, I had the pleasure of seeing and hearing that venerable old man in his 90th year, and even then, the calmness, the force, the perspicuity of his sermon, sanctified and adorned by the wisdom of grey hairs, and the authority of virtue, had such an effect upon my mind, that I never see a hoary-headed clergyman, without thinking of Mr. Walker. . . . He allowed no dissenter or methodist to interfere in the instruction of the souls committed to his care: and so successful were his exertions, that he had not one dissenter of any denomination whatever in the whole parish. — Though he avoided all religious controversies, yet when age had silvered his head, and virtuous piety had secured to his appearance reverence and silent honour, no one, however determined in his hatred of apostolic descent, could have listened to his discourse on ecclesiastical history and ancient times, without thinking that one of the beloved apostles had returned to mortality, and in that vale of peace had come to

exemplify the beauty of holiness in the life and character of Mr. Walker.

.   .   .   .

"Until the sickness of his wife, a few months previous
to her death, his health and spirits and faculties were
unimpaired. But this misfortune gave him such a shock
that his constitution gradually decayed. His senses,
except sight, still preserved their powers. He never
preached with steadiness after his wife's death. His
voice faltered: he always looked at the seat she had used.
He could not pass her tomb without tears. He became,
when alone, sad and melancholy, though still among his
friends kind and good-humoured. He went to bed
about twelve o'clock the night before his death. As
his custom was, he went, tottering and leaning upon his
daughter's arm, to examine the heavens, and meditate
a few moments in the open air. 'How clear the moon
shines to-night!' He said these words, sighed, and laid
down. At six next morning he was found a corpse.
Many a tear, and many a heavy heart, and many a
grateful blessing followed him to the grave."

Having mentioned in this narrative the vale of
Loweswater as a place where Mr. Walker taught school,
I will add a few memoranda from its parish register,
respecting a person apparently of desires as moderate,
with whom he must have been intimate during his residence there.

"Let him that would, ascend the tottering seat
Of courtly grandeur, and become as great

Dove Cottage

> As are his mounting wishes; but for me,
> Let sweet repose and rest my portion be.
>
> HENRY FOREST, Curate."

> "Honour, the idol which the most adore,
> Receives no homage from my knee;
> Content in privacy I value more
> Than all uneasy dignity."

"Henry Forest came to Loweswater, 1708, being 25 years of age."

"This curacy was twice augmented by Queen Anne's Bounty. The first payment, with great difficulty, was paid to Mr. John Curwen of London, on the 9th of May, 1724, deposited by me, Henry Forest, Curate of Loweswater. Y^e said 9th of May, ye said Mr. Curwen went to the office, and saw my name registered there, &c. This, by the Providence of God, came by lot to this poor place.

> "Hæc testor H. Forest."

In another place he records that the sycamore trees were planted in the churchyard in 1710.

He died in 1741, having been curate thirty-four years. It is not improbable that H. Forest was the gentleman who assisted Robert Walker in his classical studies at Loweswater.

To this parish register is prefixed a motto, of which the following verses are a part: —

> "Invigilate viri, tacito nam tempora gressu
> Diffugiunt, nulloque sono convertitur annus;
> Utendum est ætate, cito pede præterit ætas."

38.   "And feel that I am happier than I know."

                                              Milton.

The allusion to the Greek Poet will be obvious to the classical reader.

39.   —— "awhile the living hill
      Heaved with convulsive throes, and all was still."

                                              Dr. Darwin.

40. During the month of December 1820, I accompanied a much-beloved and honoured Friend in a walk through different parts of his estate, with a view to fix upon the site of a new Church which he intended to erect. It was one of the most beautiful mornings of a mild season, — our feelings were in harmony with the cherishing influences of the scene; and such being our purpose, we were naturally led to look back upon past events with wonder and gratitude, and on the future with hope. Not long afterwards, some of the Sonnets which will be found towards the close of this series were produced as a private memorial of that morning's occupation.

The Catholic Question, which was agitated in Parliament about that time, kept my thoughts in the same course; and it struck me that certain points in the Ecclesiastical History of our Country might advantageously be presented to view in verse. Accordingly, I took up the subject, and what I now offer to the reader was the result.

When this work was far advanced, I was agreeably surprised to find that my friend, Mr. Southey, had been engaged with similar views in writing a concise History of the Church *in* England. If our Productions, thus unintentionally coinciding, shall be found to illustrate each other, it will prove a high gratification to me, which I am sure my friend will participate.

W. WORDSWORTH.

RYDAL MOUNT, *January 24, 1822.*

For the convenience of passing from one point of the subject to another without shocks of abruptness, this work has taken the shape of a series of Sonnets: but the Reader, it is to be hoped, will find that the pictures are often so closely connected as to have jointly the effect of passages of a poem in a form of stanza to which there is no objection but one that bears upon the Poet only — its difficulty.

41. Stillingfleet adduces many arguments in support of this opinion, but they are unconvincing. The latter part of this Sonnet refers to a favourite notion of Roman Catholic writers, that Joseph of Arimathea and his companions brought Christianity into Britain, and built a rude church at Glastonbury; alluded to hereafter, in a passage upon the dissolution of monasteries.

42. This water-fowl was, among the Druids, an emblem of those traditions connected with the Deluge that made an important part of their mysteries. The Cormorant was a bird of bad omen.

43. This hill at St. Alban's must have been an object of great interest to the imagination of the venerable

Bede, who thus describes it, with a delicate feeling, delightful to meet with in that rude age, traces of which are frequent in his works: "Variis herbarum floribus depictus imò usquequaque vestitus, in quo nihil repentè, arduum, nihil præceps, nihil abruptum, quem lateribus longè latèque deductum in modum æquoris natura complanat, dignum videlicet eum pro insitâ sibi specie venustatis jam olim reddens, qui beati martyris cruore dicaretur."

44. Alluding to the victory gained under Germanus. — See Bede.

45. The last six lines of this Sonnet are chiefly from the prose of Daniel; and here I will state (though to the Readers whom this Poem will chiefly interest it is unnecessary) that my obligations to other prose writers are frequent, — obligations which, even if I had not a pleasure in courting, it would have been presumptuous to shun, in treating an historical subject. I must, however, particularise Fuller, to whom I am indebted in the Sonnet upon Wicliffe and in other instances. And upon the acquittal of the Seven Bishops I have done little more than versify a lively description of that event in the MS. Memoirs of the first Lord Lonsdale.

46. "Ethelforth reached the convent of Bangor, he perceived the Monks, twelve hundred in number, offering prayers for the success of their countrymen: 'If they are praying against us,' he exclaimed, 'they are fighting against us'; and he ordered them to be first attacked: they were destroyed; and, appalled by

their fate, the courage of Brocmail wavered, and he fled from the field in dismay. Thus abandoned by their leader, his army soon gave way, and Ethelforth obtained a decisive conquest. Ancient Bangor itself soon fell into his hands, and was demolished; the noble monastery was levelled to the ground; its library, which is mentioned as a large one, the collection of ages, the repository of the most precious monuments of the ancient Britons, was consumed; half-ruined walls, gates, and rubbish were all that remained of the magnificent edifice." — See Turner's valuable history of the Anglo-Saxons.

Taliesin was present at the battle which preceded this desolation.

The account Bede gives of this remarkable event suggests a most striking warning against National and Religious prejudices.

47. The person of Paulinus is thus described by Bede, from the memory of an eye-witness: "Longæ staturæ, paululum incurvus, nigro capillo, facie macilentâ, naso adunco, pertenui, venerabilis simul et terribilis aspectu."

48. See the original of this speech in Bede. — The Conversion of Edwin, as related by him, is highly interesting — and the breaking up of this Council accompanied with an event so striking and characteristic, that I am tempted to give it at length in a translation. "Who, exclaimed the King, when the Council was ended, shall first desecrate the altars and the temples? I,

answered the Chief Priest; for who more fit than myself, through the wisdom which the true God hath given
me, to destroy, for the good example of others, what in
foolishness I worshipped? Immediately, casting away
vain superstition, he besought the King to grant him
what the laws did not allow to a priest, arms and a courser
(equum emissarium); which mounting, and furnished
with a sword and lance, he proceeded to destroy the
Idols. The crowd, seeing this, thought him mad — he,
however, halted not, but, approaching, he profaned
the temple, casting against it the lance which he had
held in his hand, and, exulting in acknowledgment of the
worship of the true God, he ordered his companions to
pull down the temple, with all its enclosures. The place
is shown where those idols formerly stood, not far
from York, at the source of the river Derwent, and is
at this day called Gormund Gaham, ubi pontifex ille,
inspirante Deo vero, polluit ac destruxit eas, *quas
ipse sacraverat aras*." The last expression is a pleasing
proof that the venerable monk of Wearmouth was familiar with the poetry of Virgil.

49. The early propagators of Christianity were accustomed to preach near rivers, for the convenience
of baptism.

50. Having spoken of the zeal, disinterestedness,
and temperance of the clergy of those times, Bede
thus proceeds: "Unde et in magna erat veneratione
tempore illo religionis habitus, ita ut ubicunque cleri-
cus aliquis, aut monachus adveniret, gaudenter ab

omnibus tanquam Dei famulus exciperetur. Etiam si in itinere pergens inveniretur, accurrebant, et flexâ, cervice, vel manu signari, vel ore illius se benedicti, gaudebant. Verbis quoque horum exhortatoriis diligenter auditum præbebant."—Lib. iii, cap. 26.

51. He expired dictating the last words of a translation of St. John's Gospel.

52. See, in Turner's History, vol. iii, p. 528, the account of the erection of Ramsey Monastery. Penances were removable by the performance of acts of charity and benevolence.

53. Through the whole of his life, Alfred was subject to grievous maladies.

54. The violent measures carried on under the influence of *Dunstan*, for strengthening the Benedictine Order, were a leading cause of the second series of Danish invasions. — *See Turner.*

55. Which is still extant.

56. The decision of the Council was believed to be instantly known in remote parts of Europe.

57. "Bonum est nos hic esse, quia homo vivit purius, cadit rarius, surgit velocius, incedit cautius, quiescit securius, moritur felicius, purgatur citius, præmiatur copiosius." — BERNARD. "This sentence," says Dr. Whitaker, "is usually inscribed in some conspicuous part of the Cistertian houses."

58. The list of foul names bestowed upon those poor creatures is long and curious; — and, as is, alas! too natural, most of the opprobious appellations are drawn

from circumstances into which they were forced by their persecutors, who even consolidated their miseries into one reproachful term, calling them Patarenians, or Paturins, from *pati*, to suffer.

> "Dwellers with wolves, she names them, for the pine
> And green oak are their covert; as the gloom
> Of night oft foils their enemy's design,
> She calls them Riders on the flying broom
> Sorcerers, whose frame and aspect have become
> One and the same through practices malign."

59. These two lines are adopted from a MS., written about the year 1770, which accidentally fell into my possession. The close of the preceding Sonnet on monastic voluptuousness is taken from the same source, as is the verse, "Where Venus sits," etc., and the line, "Once ye were holy, ye are holy still," in a subsequent Sonnet.

60. "M. Latimer suffered his keeper very quietly to pull off his hose, and his other array, which to looke unto was very simple: and being stripped into his shrowd, he seemed as comely a person to them that were present, as one should lightly see: and whereas in his clothes hee appeared a withered and crooked sillie (weak) olde man, he now stood bolt upright, as comely a father as one might lightly behold. . . . Then they brought a faggotte, kindled with fire, and laid the same downe at doctor Ridley's feete. To whome M. Latimer spake in this manner, 'Bee of good comfort, master Ridley, and play the man: wee shall this day light such

a candle by God's grace in England, as I trust shall never be put out.'" — *Fox's Acts*, etc.

Similar alterations in the outward figure and deportment of persons brought to like trial were not uncommon. See note to the above passage in Dr. Wordsworth's *Ecclesiastical Biography*, for an example in an humble Welsh fisherman.

61. For the belief in this fact, see the contemporary historians.

62. "On foot they went, and took Salisbury in their way, purposely to see the good Bishop, who made Mr. Hooker sit at his own table; which Mr. Hooker boasted of with much joy and gratitude when he saw his mother and friends; and at the Bishop's parting with him, the Bishop gave him good counsel and his benediction, but forgot to give him money; which when the Bishop had considered, he sent a servant in all haste to call Richard back to him, and at Richard's return, the Bishop said to him, 'Richard, I sent for you back to lend you a horse which hath carried me many a mile, and I thank God with much ease,' and presently delivered into his hand a walking-staff, with which he professed he had travelled through many parts of Germany; and he said, 'Richard, I do not give, but lend you my horse; be sure you be honest, and bring my horse back to me, at your return this way to Oxford. And I do now give you ten groats to bear your charges to Exeter; and here is ten groats more, which I charge you to deliver to your mother, and tell her I send her a Bishop's benediction with it,

and beg the continuance of her prayers for me. And if you bring my horse back to me, I will give you ten groats more to carry you on foot to the college; and so God bless you, good Richard.'" — See *Walton's Life of Richard Hooker.*

63. A common device in religious and political conflicts. — See Strype, in support of this instance.

64. The Jung-frau.

65. In this age a word cannot be said in praise of Laud, or even in compassion for his fate, without incurring a charge of bigotry; but fearless of such imputation, I concur with Hume, "that it is sufficient for his vindication to observe that his errors were the most excusable of all those which prevailed during that zealous period." A key to the right understanding of those parts of his conduct that brought the most odium upon him in his own time, may be found in the following passage of his speech before the bar of the House of Peers: "Ever since I came in place, I have laboured nothing more than that the external publick worship of God, so much slighted in divers parts of this kingdom, might be preserved, and that with as much decency and uniformity as might be. For I evidently saw that the public neglect of God's service in the outward face of it, and the nasty lying of many places dedicated to that service, *had almost cast a damp upon the true and inward worship of God, which while we live in the body, needs external helps, and all little enough to keep it in any vigour.*"

66. American episcopacy, in union with the church in England, strictly belongs to the general subject; and I here make my acknowledgments to my American friends, Bishop Doane, and Mr. Henry Reed of Philadelphia, for having suggested to me the propriety of adverting to it, and pointed out the virtues and intellectual qualities of Bishop White, which so eminently fitted him for the great work he undertook. Bishop White was consecrated at Lambeth, Feb. 4, 1787, by Archbishop Moore; and before his long life was closed, twenty-six bishops had been consecrated in America by himself. For his character and opinions, see his own numerous works, and a "Sermon in commemoration of him, by George Washington Doane, Bishop of New Jersey."

67. Among the benefits arising, as Mr. Coleridge has well observed, from a Church establishment of endowments corresponding with the wealth of the country to which it belongs, may be reckoned as eminently important the examples of civility and refinement which the clergy stationed at intervals afford to the whole people. The established clergy in many parts of England have long been, as they continue to be, the principal bulwark against barbarism, and the link which unites the sequestered peasantry with the intellectual advancement of the age. Nor is it below the dignity of the subject to observe that their taste, as acting upon rural residences and scenery, often furnishes models which country gentlemen, who are more at liberty to follow the caprices of fashion, might profit by. The pre-

cincts of an old residence must be treated by ecclesiastics with respect, both from prudence and necessity. I remember being much pleased, some years ago, at Rose Castle, the rural seat of the See of Carlisle, with a style of garden and architecture which, if the place had belonged to a wealthy layman, would no doubt have been swept away. A parsonage house generally stands not far from the church; this proximity imposes favourable restraints, and sometimes suggests an affecting union of the accommodations and elegancies of life with the outward signs of piety and morality. With pleasure I recall to mind a happy instance of this in the residence of an old and much-valued Friend in Oxfordshire. The house and church stand parallel to each other, at a small distance; a circular lawn, or rather grass-plot, spreads between them; shrubs and trees curve from each side of the dwelling, veiling, but not hiding, the church. From the front of this dwelling no part of the burial-ground is seen; but as you wind by the side of the shrubs towards the steeple-end of the church, the eye catches a single, small, low, monumental headstone, moss-grown, sinking into and gently inclining towards the earth. Advance, and the churchyard, populous and gay with glittering tombstones, opens upon the view. This humble and beautiful parsonage called forth a tribute, for which see the sonnet entitled "A Parsonage in Oxfordshire," p. 602.

68. This is still continued in many churches in Westmoreland. It takes place in the month of July, when the

floor of the stalls is strewn with fresh rushes; and hence it is called the "Rush-bearing."

69. This is borrowed from an affecting passage in Mr. George Dyer's history of Cambridge.

70. See Burnet, who is unusually animated on this subject; the east wind, so anxiously expected and prayed for, was called the "Protestant wind."

71. The Lutherans have retained the Cross within their churches: it is to be regretted that we have not done the same.

72. Some say that Monte Rosa takes its name from a belt of rock at its summit — a very unpoetical and scarcely a probable supposition.

VOLUME VIII

1. Bekangs Ghyll — or the dell of nightshade — in which stands St. Mary's Abbey in Low Furness.

2. Glen Myrv.

3. Here and infra, see Forsyth.

4. Countess of Winchilsea.

5. The river Rotha, that flows into Windermere from the lakes of Grasmere and Rydal.

6. This Sonnet, as Poetry, explains itself, yet the scene of the incident having been a wild wood, it may be doubted, as a point of natural history, whether the bird was aware that his attentions were bestowed upon a human, or even a living creature. But a Redbreast will perch upon the foot of a gardener at work, and

alight on the handle of the spade when his hand is half upon it — this I have seen. And under my own roof I have witnessed affecting instances of the creature's friendly visits to the chambers of sick persons, as described in the verses to the Redbreast, vol. ix, p. 168. One of these welcome intruders used frequently to roost upon a nail in the wall, from which a picture had hung, and was ready, as morning came, to pipe his song in the hearing of the Invalid, who had been long confined to her room. These attachments to a particular person, when marked and continued, used to be reckoned ominous; but the superstition is passing away.

7. This line alludes to Sonnets which will be found in another Class.

8. See Waterton's *Wanderings in South America.*

9. "In the Vale of Grasmere, by the side of the old high-way leading to Ambleside, is a gate which, time out of mind, has been called the Wishing-gate."

Having been told, upon what I thought good authority, that this gate had been destroyed, and the opening, where it hung, walled up, I gave vent immediately to my feelings in these stanzas. But going to the place some time after, I found, with much delight, my old favourite unmolested.

10. There is now, alas! no possibility of the anticipation, with which the above Epistle concludes, being realised: nor were the verses ever seen by the Individual for whom they were intended. She accompanied her husband, the Rev. Wm. Fletcher, to India, and died of

cholera, at the age of thirty-two or thirty-three years, on her way from Shalapore to Bombay, deeply lamented by all who knew her.

Her enthusiasm was ardent, her piety steadfast; and her great talents would have enabled her to be eminently useful in the difficult path of life to which she had been called. The opinion she entertained of her own per-formances, given to the world under her maiden name, Jewsbury, was modest and humble, and, indeed, far below their merits; as is often the case with those who are making trial of their powers, with a hope to discover what they are best fitted for. In one quality, viz., quickness in the motions of her mind, she had, within the range of the Author's acquaintance, no equal.

11. I am indebted, here, to a passage in one of Mr. Digby's valuable works.

12. See, in Percy's *Reliques*, that fine old ballad, "The Spanish Lady's Love"; from which Poem the form of stanza, as suitable to dialogue, is adopted.

13. Peter Henry Bruce, having given in his enter-taining Memoirs the substance of this Tale, affirms that, besides the concurring reports of others, he had the story from the lady's own mouth.

The Lady Catherine, mentioned towards the close, is the famous Catherine, then bearing that name as the acknowledged Wife of Peter the Great.

14. In Gaelic, Buchaill Eite.

15. This sonnet describes the *exterior* of a Highland hut, as often seen under a morning or evening sunshine.

To the authoress of the "Address to the Wind," and other poems, in this volume, who was my fellow-traveller in this tour, I am indebted for the following extract from her journal, which accurately describes, under particular circumstances, the beautiful appearance of the *interior* of one of these rude habitations.

"On our return from the Trosachs the evening began to darken, and it rained so heavily that we were completely wet before we had come two miles, and it was dark when we landed with our boatman, at his hut upon the banks of Loch Katrine. I was faint from cold: the good woman had provided, according to her promise, a better fire than we had found in the morning; and, indeed, when I had sat down in the chimney-corner of her smoky biggin, I thought I had never felt more comfortable in my life: a pan of coffee was boiling for us, and having put our clothes in the way of drying, we all sat down thankful for shelter. We could not prevail upon our boatman, the master of the house, to draw near the fire, though he was cold and wet, or to suffer his wife to get him dry clothes till she had served us, which she did most willingly, though not very expeditiously.

"A Cumberland man of the same rank would not have had such a notion of what was fit and right in his own house, or, if he had, one would have accused him of servility; but in the Highlander it only seemed like politeness (however erroneous and painful to us), naturally growing out of the dependence of the inferiors

of the clan upon their laird; he did not, however, refuse to let his wife bring out the whiskey bottle for his
refreshment, at our request. 'She keeps a dram,' as the
phrase is: indeed, I believe there is scarcely a lonely
house by the wayside, in Scotland, where travellers
may not be accommodated with a dram. We asked for
sugar, butter, barley-bread, and milk: and, with a
smile and a stare more of kindness than wonder, she
replied, 'Ye'll get that,' bringing each article separately.
We caroused our cups of coffee, laughing like children
at the strange atmosphere in which we were: the smoke
came in gusts, and spread along the walls; and above our
heads in the chimney (where the hens were roosting) it
appeared like clouds in the sky. We laughed and laughed
again, in spite of the smarting of our eyes, yet had a
quieter pleasure in observing the beauty of the beams
and rafters gleaming between the clouds of smoke: they
had been crusted over and varnished by many winters,
till, where the firelight fell upon them, they had become as glossy as black rocks, on a sunny day, cased in
ice. When we had eaten our supper we sat about half
an hour, and I think I never felt so deeply the blessing
of a hospitable welcome and a warm fire. The man of the
house repeated from time to time that we should often
tell of this night when we got to our homes, and inter-
posed praises of his own lake, which he had more than
once, when we were returning in the boat, ventured to
say was 'bonnier than Loch Lomond.' Our companion
from the Trosachs, who, it appeared, was an Edinburgh

drawing-master going, during the vacation, on a pedestrian tour to John O'Groat's House, was to sleep in the barn with my fellow-travellers, where the man said he had plenty of dry hay. I do not believe that the hay of the Highlands is ever very dry, but this year it had a better chance than usual: wet or dry, however, the next morning they said they had slept comfortably. When I went to bed, the mistress, desiring me to '*go ben*,' attended me with a candle, and assured me that the bed was dry, though not 'sic as I had been used to.' It was of chaff; there were two others in the room, a cupboard and two chests, upon one of which stood milk in wooden vessels covered over. The walls of the house were of stone unplastered; it consisted of three apartments, the cow-house at one end, the kitchen or house in the middle, and the spence at the other end; the rooms were divided, not up to the rigging, but only to the beginning of the roof, so that there was a free passage for light and smoke from one end of the house to the other. I went to bed some time before the rest of the family; the door was shut between us, and they had a bright fire, which I could not see, but the light it sent up amongst the varnished rafters and beams, which crossed each other in almost as intricate and fantastic a manner as I have seen the under-boughs of a large beech-tree withered by the depth of shade above, produced the most beautiful effect that can be conceived. It was like what I should suppose an underground cave or temple to be with a dripping or moist roof, and the moonlight entering in upon it by some means or other; and yet the colours were more like those of melted gems. I lay looking up till the light of the fire faded away, and the man and his wife and child had crept into their bed at the other end of the room; I did not sleep much, but passed a comfortable night; for my bed, though hard, was warm and clean: the unusualness of my situation prevented me from sleeping. I could hear the waves beat against the shore of the lake; a little rill close to the door made a much louder noise, and, when I sat up in my bed, I could see the lake through an open window-place at the bed's head. Add to this, it rained all night. I was less occupied by remembrance of the Trosachs, beautiful as they were, than the vision of the Highland hut, which I could not get out of my head; I thought of the Faery-land of Spenser, and what I had read in romance at other times; and then what a feast it would be for a London Pantomime-maker could he but transplant it to Drury-lane, with all its beautiful colours!" — *MS.*

16. The following is from the same MS., and gives an account of the visit to Bothwell Castle here alluded to: —

"It was exceedingly delightful to enter thus unexpectedly upon such a beautiful region. The castle stands nobly, overlooking the Clyde. When we came up to it, I was hurt to see that flower-borders had taken place of the natural overgrowings of the ruin, the scattered stones, and wild plants. It is a large and grand pile of red freestone, harmonising perfectly with the rocks of the river, from which, no doubt, it has been hewn. When I was a little accustomed to the unnaturalness of a modern garden, I could not help admiring the excessive beauty and luxuriance of some of the plants, particularly the purple-flowered clematis, and a broad-leafed creeping plant without flowers, which scrambled up the castle wall, along with the ivy, and spread its vine-like branches so lavishly that it seemed to be in its natural situation, and one could not help thinking that, though not self-planted among the ruins of this country, it must somewhere have its native abode in such places. If Bothwell Castle had not been close to the Douglas mansion, we should have been disgusted with the possessor's miserable conception of *adorning* such a venerable ruin; but it is so very near to the house, that of necessity the pleasure-grounds must have extended beyond it, and perhaps the neatness of a shaven lawn, and the complete desolation natural to a ruin, might have made an unpleasing contrast; and, besides being within the precincts of the pleasure-grounds, and so very near to the dwelling of a noble family, it has forfeited, in some degree, its independent majesty, and becomes a tributary to the mansion: its solitude being interrupted, it has no longer the command over the mind in sending it back into past times, or excluding the ordinary feelings which we bear about us in daily life. We had then only to regret that the castle and the house were so near to each other; and it was impossible *not* to regret it; for the ruin presides in state over the

river, far from city or town, as if it might have a peculiar privilege to preserve its memorials of past ages,
and maintain its own character for centuries to come.
We sat upon a bench under the high trees, and had
beautiful views of the different reaches of the river,
above and below.   On the opposite bank, which is
finely wooded with elms and other trees, are the remains of a priory built upon a rock; and rock and ruin
are so blended, that it is impossible to separate the one
from the other. Nothing can be more beautiful than
the little remnant of this holy place; elm-trees (for we
were near enough to distinguish them by their branches)
grow out of the walls, and overshadow a small, but
very elegant window. It can scarcely be conceived what
a grace the castle and priory impart to each other; and
the river Clyde flows on, smooth and unruffled, below,
seeming to my thoughts more in harmony with the
sober and stately images of former times, than if it had
roared over a rocky channel, forcing its sound upon the
ear. It blended gently with the warbling of the smaller
birds, and the chattering of the larger ones that had
made their nests in the ruins. In this fortress the chief
of the English nobility were confined after the battle
of Bannockburn. If a man *is* to be a prisoner, he scarcely
could have a more pleasant place to solace his captivity;
but I thought that, for close confinement, I should prefer
the banks of a lake, or the seaside. The greatest charm
of a brook or river is in the liberty to pursue it through
its windings; you can then take it in whatever mood

you like; silent or noisy, sportive or quiet. The beauties of a brook or river must be sought, and the pleasure is in going in search of them; those of a lake or of the sea come to you of themselves. These rude warriors cared little, perhaps, about either; and yet, if one may judge from the writings of Chaucer and from the old romances, more interesting passions were connected with natural objects in the days of chivalry than now; though going in search of scenery, as it is called, had not then been thought of. I had previously heard nothing of Bothwell Castle, at least nothing that I remembered; therefore, perhaps, my pleasure was greater, compared with what I received elsewhere, than others might feel." — *MS. Journal.*

17. "In the time of the first Robert de Clifford, in the year 1333 or 1334, Edward Baliol king of Scotland came into Westmoreland, and stayed some time with the said Robert at his castles of Appleby, Brougham, and Pendragon. And during that time they ran a stag by a single greyhound out of Whinfell Park to Red-kirk, in Scotland, and back again to this place; where, being both spent, the stag leaped over the pales, but died on the other side; and the greyhound, attempting to leap, fell, and died on the contrary side. In memory of this fact the stag's horns were nailed upon a tree just by, and (the dog being named Hercules) this rhythm was made upon them: —

> 'Hercules killed Hart a greese,
> And Hart a greese killed Hercules.'

The tree to this day bears the name of Hart's-horn Tree. The horns in process of time were almost grown over by the growth of the tree, and another pair was put up in their place." — NICHOLSON AND BURNS'S *History of Westmoreland and Cumberland.*

The tree has now disappeared, but I well remember its imposing appearance as it stood, in a decayed state, by the side of the highroad leading from Penrith to Appleby. This whole neighbourhood abounds in interesting traditions and vestiges of antiquity, viz., Julian's Bower; Brougham and Penrith Castles; Penrith Beacon, and the curious remains in Penrith Churchyard; Arthur's Round Table, and, close by, Maybrough; the excavation, called the Giant's Cave, on the banks of the Emont; Long Meg and her Daughters, near Eden, etc.

18. How much the Broach is sometimes prized by persons in humble stations may be gathered from an occurrence mentioned to me by a female friend. She had had an opportunity of benefiting a poor old woman in her own hut, who, wishing to make a return, said to her daughter, in Erse, in a tone of plaintive earnestness, "I would give anything I have, but I *hope* she does not wish for my Broach!" and, uttering these words, she put her hand upon the Broach which fastened her kerchief, and which, she imagined, had attracted the eye of her benefactress.

19. Many years ago, when I was at Greta Bridge, in Yorkshire, the hostess of the inn, proud of her skill in etymology, said, that "the name of the river was taken

from the *bridge*, the form of which, as every one must notice, exactly resembled a great A." Dr. Whitaker has derived it from the word of common occurrence in the north of England, "*to greet*"; signifying to lament aloud, mostly with weeping: a conjecture rendered more probable from the stony and rocky channel of both the Cumberland and Yorkshire rivers. The Cumberland Greta, though it does not, among the country people, take up *that* name till within three miles of its disappearance in the river Derwent, may be considered as having its source in the mountain cove of Wythburn, and thence flowing through Thirlmere. The beautiful features of that lake are known only to those who, travelling between Grasmere and Keswick, have quitted the main road in the vale of Wythburn, and, crossing over to the opposite side of the lake, have proceeded with it on the right hand.

The channel of the Greta, immediately above Keswick, has, for the purposes of building, been in a great measure cleared of the immense stones which, by their concussion in high floods, produced the loud and awful noises described in the sonnet.

"The scenery upon this river," says Mr. Southey in his Colloquies, "where it passes under the woody side of Latrigg, is of the finest and most remembrable kind:

'— ambiguo lapsu refluitque fluitque,
Occurrensque sibi venturas aspicit undas.'"

20. Attached to the church of Brigham was formerly a chantry, which held a moiety of the manor; and in

the decayed parsonage some vestiges of monastic architecture are still to be seen.

21. "The fears and impatience of Mary were so great," says Robertson, "that she got into a fisher-boat, and with about twenty attendants landed at Workington, in Cumberland; and thence she was conducted with many marks of respect to Carlisle." The apartment in which the Queen had slept at Workington Hall (where she was received by Sir Henry Curwen, as became her rank and misfortunes) was long preserved, out of respect to her memory, as she had left it; and one cannot but regret that some necessary alterations in the mansion could not be effected without its destruction.

22. St. Bees' Heads, anciently called the Cliff of Baruth, are a conspicuous sea-mark for all vessels sailing in the N.E. parts of the Irish Sea. In a bay, one side of which is formed by the southern headland, stands the village of St. Bees; a place distinguished, from very early times, for its religious and scholastic foundations.

"St. Bees," say Nicholson and Burns, "had its name from Bega, an holy woman from Ireland, who is said to have founded here, about the year of our Lord 650, a small monastery, where afterwards a church was built in memory of her.

"The aforesaid religious house, being destroyed by the Danes, was restored by William de Meschiens, son of Ranulph, and brother of Ranulph de Meschiens, first Earl of Cumberland after the Conquest; and made a cell of a prior and six Benedictine monks to the Abbey of St. Mary at York."

Several traditions of miracles, connected with the foundation of the first of these religious houses, survive among the people of the neighbourhood; one of which is alluded to in these Stanzas; and another, of a somewhat bolder and more peculiar character, has furnished the subject of a spirited poem by the Rev. R. Parkinson, M.A., late Divinity Lecturer of St. Bees' College, and now Fellow of the Collegiate Church of Manchester.

After the dissolution of the monasteries, Archbishop Grindal founded a free school at St. Bees, from which the counties of Cumberland and Westmoreland have derived great benefit; and recently, under the patronage of the Earl of Lonsdale, a college has been established there for the education of ministers for the English Church. The old Conventual Church has been repaired under the superintendence of the Rev. Dr. Ainger, the Head of the College, and is well worthy of being visited by any strangers who might be led to the neighbourhood of this celebrated spot.

The form of stanza in this Poem, and something in the style of versification, are adopted from the "St. Monica," a poem of much beauty upon a monastic subject, by Charlotte Smith: a lady to whom English verse is under greater obligations than are likely to be either acknowledged or remembered. She wrote little, and that little unambitiously, but with true feeling for rural Nature, at a time when Nature was not much regarded by English Poets; for in point of time her earlier writings preceded, I believe, those of Cowper and Burns.

23. I am aware that I am here treading upon tender ground; but to the intelligent reader I feel that no apology is due. The prayers of survivors, during passionate grief for the recent loss of relatives and friends, as the object of those prayers could no longer be the suffering body of the dying, would naturally be ejaculated for the souls of the departed; the barriers between the two worlds dissolving before the power of love and faith. The ministers of religion, from their habitual attendance upon sick-beds, would be daily witnesses of these benign results; and hence would be strongly tempted to aim at giving to them permanence, by embodying them in rites and ceremonies, recurring at stated periods. All this, as it was in course of nature, so was it blameless, and even praiseworthy; some of its effects, in that rude state of society, could not but be salutary. No reflecting person, however, can view without sorrow the abuses which rose out of thus formalising sublime instincts, and disinterested movements of passion, and perverting them into means of gratifying the ambition and rapacity of the priesthood. But, while we deplore and are indignant at these abuses, it would be a great mistake if we imputed the origin of the offices to prospective selfishness on the part of the monks and clergy: *they* were at first sincere in their sympathy, and

in their degree dupes rather of their own creed, than artful and designing men. Charity is, upon the whole, the safest guide that we can take in judging our fellow-men, whether of past ages or of the present time.

24. See "The Excursion," seventh part, and "Ecclesiastical Sonnets," second part, near the beginning.

25. The Tower of Refuge, an ornament to Douglas Bay, was erected chiefly through the humanity and zeal of Sir William Hillary; and he also was the founder of the lifeboat establishment at that place, by which, under his superintendence, and often by his exertions at the imminent hazard of his own life, many seamen and passengers have been saved.

26. The sea-water on the coast of the Isle of Man is singularly pure and beautiful.

27. This unpretending sonnet is by a gentleman nearly connected with me, and I hope, as it falls so easily into its place, that both the writer and the reader will excuse its appearance here.

28. Rushen Abbey.

29. The summit of this mountain is well chosen by Cowley as the scene of the "Vision," in which the spectral angel discourses with him concerning the government of Oliver Cromwell. "I found myself," says he, "on the top of that famous hill in the Island Mona, which has the prospect of three great, and not long since most happy, kingdoms. As soon as ever I looked upon them, they called forth the sad representation of all the sins and all the miseries that had over-

whelmed them these twenty years." It is not to be
denied that the changes now in progress, and the passions, and the way in which they work, strikingly resemble those which led to the disasters the philosophic
writer so feelingly bewails. God grant that the resemblance may not become still more striking as months and
years advance!

30. This ingenious piece of workmanship, as I afterwards learned, had been executed for their own amusement by some labourers employed about the place.

31. The reader may be tempted to exclaim, "How
came this and the two following sonnets to be written,
after the dissatisfaction expressed in the preceding
one?" In fact, at the risk of incurring the reasonable
displeasure of the master of the steamboat, I returned
to the cave, and explored it under circumstances more
favourable to those imaginative impressions which it is
so wonderfully fitted to make upon the mind.

32. Upon the head of the columns which form the
front of the cave rests a body of decomposed basaltic
matter, which was richly decorated with that large
bright flower, the ox-eyed daisy. I had noticed the
same flower growing with profusion among the bold
rocks on the western coast of the Isle of Man; making a brilliant contrast with their black and gloomy
surfaces.

33. The four last lines of this sonnet are adopted
from a well-known sonnet of Russel, as conveying my
feeling better than any words of my own could do.

34. It is to be feared that there is more of the poet than the sound etymologist in this derivation of the name Eden. On the western coast of Cumberland is a rivulet which enters the sea at Moresby, known also in the neighbourhood by the name of Eden. May not the latter syllable come from the word Dean, *a valley?* Langdale, near Ambleside, is by the inhabitants called Langden. The former syllable occurs in the name Emont, a principal feeder of the Eden; and the stream which flows, when the tide is out, over Cartmel Sands, is called the Ea—eau, French — aqua, Latin.

35. The chain of Crossfell.

36. At Corby, a few miles below Nunnery, the Eden is crossed by a magnificent viaduct; and another of these works is thrown over a deep glen or ravine at a very short distance from the main stream.

37. The daughters of Long Meg, placed in a perfect circle eighty yards in diameter, are seventy-two in number above ground; a little way out of the circle stands Long Meg herself, a single stone, eighteen feet high. When I first saw this monument, as I came on it by surprise, I might overrate its importance as an object; but, though it will not bear a comparison with Stonehenge, I must say, I have not seen any other relique of those dark ages which can pretend to rival it in singularity and dignity of appearance.

38. This sonnet was written immediately after certain trials took place at the Cumberland Assizes, when the Earl of Lonsdale, in consequence of repeated and long-

continued attacks upon his character through the local press, had thought it right to prosecute the conductors and proprietors of three several journals. A verdict of libel was given in one case; and, in the others, the prosecutions were withdrawn, upon the individuals retracting and disavowing the charges, expressing regret that they had been made, and promising to abstain from the like in future.

39. A pleasure-house built by the late Duke of Norfolk upon the banks of Ullswater. "Force" is the word used in the Lake District for Waterfall.

VOLUME IX

1. The words —

> "Matthew, Mark, and Luke, and John,
> Bless the bed that I lie on,"

are part of a child's prayer, still in general use throughout the Northern counties.

2. The pile of buildings composing the palace and convent of San Lorenzo has, in common usage, lost its proper name in that of the *Escurial*, a village at the foot of the hill upon which the splendid edifice, built by Philip the Second, stands. It need scarcely be added, that Wilkie is the painter alluded to.

3. In the class entitled "Musings" in Mr. Southey's Minor Poems is one upon his own miniature Picture, taken in childhood, and another upon a landscape painted by Gaspar Poussin. It is possible that every

word of the above verses, though similar in subject, might have been written had the author been unacquainted with those beautiful effusions of poetic sentiment. But, for his own satisfaction, he must be allowed thus publicly to acknowledge the pleasure those two Poems of his Friend have given him, and the grateful influence they have upon his mind as often as he reads them, or thinks of them.

4. This way of indicating the *name* of my lamented friend has been found fault with; perhaps rightly so; but I may say in justification of the double sense of the word, that similar allusions are not uncommon in epitaphs. One of the best in our language in verse I ever read, was upon a person who bore the name of Palmer; and the course of the thought, throughout, turned upon the Life of the Departed, considered as a pilgrimage. Nor can I think that the objection in the present case will have much force with any one who remembers Charles Lamb's beautiful sonnet addressed to his own name, and ending —

" No deed of mine shall shame thee, gentle name! "

5. Walter Scott . . . . . . died Sept. 21, 1832
  S. T. Coleridge . . . . . " July 25, 1834
  Charles Lamb . . . . . . " Dec. 27, 1834
  Geo. Crabbe . . . . . " Feb. 3, 1832
  Felicia Hemans . . . . . " May 16, 1835

6. These words were quoted to me from "Yarrow Unvisited" by Sir Walter Scott when I visited him at

Abbotsford, a day or two before his departure for Italy; and the affecting condition in which he was when he looked upon Rome from the Janicular Mount, was reported to me by a lady who had the honour of conducting him thither.

7. If any English reader should be desirous of knowing how far I am justified in thus describing the epitaphs of Chiabrera, he will find translated specimens of them on pages 198–206 of vol. v.

8. It would be ungenerous not to advert to the religious movement that, since the composition of these verses in 1837, has made itself felt, more or less strongly, throughout the English Church; — a movement that takes, for its first principle, a devout deference to the voice of Christian antiquity. It is not my office to pass judgment on questions of theological detail; but my own repugnance to the spirit and system of Romanism has been so repeatedly and, I trust, feelingly expressed, that I shall not be suspected of a leaning that way, if I do not join in the grave charge, thrown out, perhaps in the heat of controversy, against the learned and pious men to whose labours I allude. I speak apart from controversy; but, with strong faith in the moral temper which would elevate the present by doing reverence to the past, I would draw cheerful auguries for the English Church from this movement, as likely to restore among us a tone of piety more earnest and real than that produced by the mere formalities of the understanding, refusing, in a degree which I cannot but

lament, that its own temper and judgment shall be controlled by those of antiquity.

9. Within a couple of hours of my arrival at Rome, I saw from Monte Pincio the Pine tree as described in the Sonnet; and, while expressing admiration at the beauty of its appearance, I was told by an acquaintance of my fellow-traveller, who happened to join us at the moment, that a price had been paid for it by the late Sir G. Beaumont, upon condition that the proprietor should not act upon his known intention of cutting it down.

10. Quem virum —— lyra ——
—— sumes celebrare Clio ?

11. Sanguinetto.

12. This famous sanctuary was the original establishment of Saint Romualdo (or Rumwald, as our ancestors Saxonised the name), in the 11th century, the ground (campo) being given by Count Maldo. The Camaldolensi, however, have spread wide as a branch of Benedictines, and may therefore be classed among the *gentlemen* of the monastic orders. The society comprehends two orders, monks and hermits; symbolised by their arms, two doves drinking out of the same cup. The monastery in which the monks here reside is beautifully situated, but a large unattractive edifice, not unlike a factory. The hermitage is placed in a loftier and wider region of the forest. It comprehends between twenty and thirty distinct residences, each including for its single hermit an inclosed piece of ground and three very small apartments. There are days of indulg-

ence when the hermit may quit his cell, and when old age arrives he descends from the mountain and takes his abode among the monks.

My companion had in the year 1831 fallen in with the monk, the subject of these two sonnets, who showed him his abode among the hermits. It is from him that I received the following particulars. He was then about forty years of age, but his appearance was that of an older man. He had been a painter by profession, but on taking orders changed his name from Santi to Raffaelo, perhaps with an unconscious reference as well to the great Sanzio d'Urbino as to the archangel. He assured my friend that he had been thirteen years in the hermitage and had never known melancholy or ennui. In the little recess for study and prayer, there was a small collection of books. "I read only," said he, "books of asceticism and mystical theology." On being asked the names of the most famous mystics, he enumerated *Scaramelli, San Giovanni della Croce, St. Dionysius the Areopagite* (supposing the work which bears his name to be really his), and with peculiar emphasis *Ricardo di San Vittori*. The works of *Saint Theresa* are also in high repute among ascetics. These names may interest some of my readers.

We heard that Raffaello was then living in the convent; my friend sought in vain to renew his acquaintance with him. It was probably a day of seclusion. The reader will perceive that these sonnets were supposed to be written when he was a young man.

13. In justice to the Benedictines of Camaldoli, by whom strangers are so hospitably entertained, I feel obliged to notice that I saw among them no other figure at all resembling, in size and complexion, the two monks described in this Sonnet. What was their office, or the motive which brought them to this place of mortification, which they could not have approached without being carried in this or some other way, a feeling of delicacy prevented me from inquiring. An account has before been given of the hermitage they were about to enter. It was visited by us towards the end of the month of May; yet snow was lying thick under the pine trees, within a few yards of the gate.

14. The name of Milton is pleasingly connected with Vallombrosa in many ways. The pride with which the monk, without any previous question from me, pointed out his residence, I shall not readily forget. It may be proper here to defend the poet from a charge which has been brought against him, in respect to the passage in "Paradise Lost," where this place is mentioned. It is said, that he has erred in speaking of the trees there being deciduous, whereas they are, in fact, pines. The fault-finders are themselves mistaken; the *natural* woods of the region of Vallombrosa *are* deciduous, and spread to a great extent; those near the convent are, indeed, mostly pines; but they are avenues of trees *planted* within a few steps of each other, and thus composing large tracts of wood; plots of which are periodically cut down. The appearance of those narrow avenues, upon

steep slopes open to the sky, on account of the height which the trees attain by being *forced* to grow upwards, is often very impressive. My guide, a boy of about fourteen years old, pointed this out to me in several places.

15. See for the two *first lines*, "Stanzas composed in the Simplon Pass."

16. The Poor Robin is the small wild geranium known by that name.

17. These lines were written several years ago, when reports prevailed of cruelties committed in many parts of America, by men making a law of their own passions. A far more formidable, as being a more deliberate, mischief, has appeared among those States, which have lately broken faith with the public creditor in a manner so infamous. I cannot, however, but look at both evils under a similar relation to inherent good, and hope that the time is not distant when our brethren of the West will wipe off this stain from their name and nation.

ADDITIONAL NOTE

I am happy to add that this anticipation is already partly realised; and that the reproach addressed to the Pennsylvanians in the sonnet on page 233 is no longer applicable to them. I trust that those other States to which it may yet apply will soon follow the example now set them by Philadelphia, and redeem their credit with the world. — 1850.

18. Among ancient Trees there are few, I believe, at

least in France, so worthy of attention as an Oak which may be seen in the "Pays de Caux," about a league from Yvetot, close to the church, and in the burial-ground of Allonville.

The height of this Tree does not answer to its girth; the trunk, from the roots to the summit, forms a complete cone; and the inside of this cone is hollow throughout the whole of its height.

Such is the Oak of Allonville in its state of nature. The hand of Man, however, has endeavoured to impress upon it a character still more interesting, by adding a religious feeling to the respect which its age naturally inspires.

The lower part of its hollow trunk has been transformed into a Chapel of six or seven feet in diameter, carefully wainscoted and paved, and an open iron gate guards the humble Sanctuary.

Leading to it there is a staircase, which twists round the body of the Tree. At certain seasons of the year, divine service is performed in this Chapel.

The summit has been broken off many years, but there is a surface at the top of the trunk, of the diameter of a very large tree, and from it rises a pointed roof, covered with slates, in the form of a steeple, which is surmounted with an iron Cross, that rises in a picturesque manner from the middle of the leaves, like an ancient hermitage above the surrounding Wood.

Over the entrance to the Chapel an Inscription appears, which informs us it was erected by the Abbé du

Détroit, Curate of Allonville in the year 1696; and over a door is another, dedicating it "To our Lady of Peace."

Vide No. 14, *Saturday Magazine.*

19. The hill that rises to the south-east, above Ambleside.

20. Ambleside.

21. The degree and kind of attachment which many of the yeomanry feel to their small inheritances can scarcely be over-rated. Near the house of one of them stands a magnificent tree, which a neighbour of the man advised him to fell for profit's sake. "Fell it!" exclaimed the yeoman; "I had rather fall on my knees and worship it." It happens, I believe, that the intended railway would pass through this little property, and I hope that an apology for the answer will not be thought necessary by one who enters into the strength of the feeling.

INDEX OF FIRST LINES

[291]

INDEX OF FIRST LINES

INDEX OF FIRST LINES

INDEX OF FIRST LINES

Brugès I saw attired with golden light, vii, 135.
But Cytherea, studious to invent, vii, 44.
But here no cannon thunders to the gale, vii, 240.
But liberty, and triumphs on the Main, vii, 376.
But, to outweigh all harm, the sacred Book, vii, 320.
But, to remote Northumbria's royal Hall, vii, 267.
But what if One, through grove or flowing mead, vii, 275.
But whence came they who for the Saviour Lord, vii, 303.
By a blest Husband guided, Mary came, ix, 51.
By antique Fancy trimmed — though lowly, bred, vii, 158.
By Art's bold privilege Warrior and War-horse stand, ix, 157.
By chain yet stronger must the Soul be tied, vii, 363.
By Moscow self-devoted to a blaze, vii, 37.
By playful smiles (alas! too oft, viii, 32.
By such examples moved to unbought pains, vii, 276.
By their floating mill, v, 14.
By vain affections unenthralled, viii, 31.

Call not the royal Swede unfortunate, v, 185.
Calm as an under-current, strong to draw, vii, 347.
Calm is all nature as a resting wheel, i, 10.
Calm is the fragrant air, and loth to lose, viii, 248.
Calvert! it must not be unheard by them, v, 45.
Change me, some God, into that breathing rose! vii, 214.
Chatsworth! thy stately mansion, and the pride, viii, 193.
Child of loud-throated War! the mountain Stream, iv, 153.
Child of the clouds! remote from every taint, vii, 209.
Clarkson! it was an obstinate hill to climb, v, 65.
Closing the sacred Book which long has fed, vii, 370.
Clouds, lingering yet, extend in solid bars, v, 34.
Coldly we spake. The Saxons, overpowered, vii, 284.
Come, gentle Sleep, Death's image tho' thou art, v, 42.
Come ye — who, if (which Heaven avert!) the Land, iv, 191.
Companion ! by whose buoyant Spirit cheered, ix, 63.
Complacent Fictions were they, yet the same, ix, 87.

Dark and more dark the shades of evening fell, iv, 107.
Darkness surrounds us; seeking we are lost, vii, 257.

INDEX OF FIRST LINES

INDEX OF FIRST LINES

INDEX OF FIRST LINES

INDEX OF FIRST LINES

INDEX OF FIRST LINES

[299]

INDEX OF FIRST LINES

[300]

INDEX OF FIRST LINES

INDEX OF FIRST LINES

INDEX OF FIRST LINES

[303]

INDEX OF FIRST LINES

INDEX OF FIRST LINES

[305]

INDEX OF FIRST LINES

INDEX OF FIRST LINES

INDEX OF FIRST LINES

INDEX OF FIRST LINES

[309]

INDEX OF FIRST LINES

INDEX OF FIRST LINES

INDEX OF FIRST LINES

INDEX OF FIRST LINES

INDEX OF FIRST LINES

INDEX OF TITLES

[The titles of major works and general divisions are set in SMALL CAPITALS.]

[315]

INDEX OF TITLES

INDEX OF TITLES

[317]

INDEX OF TITLES

INDEX OF TITLES

[319]

INDEX OF TITLES

INDEX OF TITLES

[321]

INDEX OF TITLES

INDEX OF TITLES

[323]

INDEX OF TITLES

INDEX OF TITLES

[325]

INDEX OF TITLES

INDEX OF TITLES

INDEX OF TITLES

[328]

INDEX OF TITLES

INDEX OF TITLES

INDEX OF TITLES

INDEX OF TITLES

INDEX OF TITLES

[333]

INDEX OF TITLES

INDEX OF TITLES

INDEX OF TITLES

[336]

INDEX OF TITLES

INDEX OF TITLES

INDEX OF TITLES

[339]

INDEX OF TITLES